Eighth Edition

Asking the Right Questions

A Guide to Critical Thinking

M. Neil Browne

Stuart M. Keeley

Bowling Green State University

PEARSON

Prentice Hall

Upper Saddle River, New Jersey 07458

Library of Congress Cataloging-in-Publication Data

Browne, M. Neil, (date)
   Asking the right questions: a guide to critical thinking / M. Neil Browne, Stuart M.
   Keeley.—8th ed.
      p.   cm.
   Includes index.
   ISBN 0-13-220304-9
   1. Criticism.   2. Critical thinking.   I. Keeley, Stuart M., 1941   II. Title.
   PN83.B785 2007
   808—dc22   2005032905

Editorial Director: Leah Jewell
Senior Acquisitions Editor: Brad Potthoff
Editorial Assistant: Tara Culliney
Senior Marketing Manager: Windley Morley
Marketing Assistant: Kara Pottle
Production Liaison: Marianne Peters-Riordan
Assistant Manufacturing Manager: Mary Ann
   Gloriande
Art Director: Jayne Conte

Cover Design: Bruce Kenselaar
Cover Illustration/Photo: Jan Tove Johansson/
   Taxi/Getty Images
Manager, Cover Visual Research & Permissions:
   Karen Sanatar
Composition/Full-Service Project Management:
   Sowmya Balaraman/Integra Software Services
Printer/Binder: R.R. Donnelley and Sons

Credits and acknowledgments borrowed from other sources and reproduced, with permission,
in this textbook appear on appropriate page within text.

This book was set in 10/13 New Baskerville by Integra Software Services and was printed by
R.R. Donnelley and Sons.

Pearson Education Ltd
Pearson Education Singapore, Pte. Ltd
Pearson Education Canada, Ltd
Pearson Education—Japan
Pearson Education Australia PTY, Limited

Pearson Education North Asia Ltd
Pearson Educación de Mexico, S.A. de C.V.
Pearson Education Malaysia, Pte. Ltd
Pearson Education, Upper Saddle River,
   New Jersey

10 9 8 7 6 5 4 3 2 1
ISBN 0-13-220304-9

Contents

Preface

The eighth edition is our small contribution to the collective effort to highlight the benefits of careful, rational assessment of reasoning. While we are immensely pleased by the success of this book with decades of readers in many countries and languages, we cannot help but notice the immense disrespect for evidence, sloppy use of language, and substitution of hollering for reason in so much of our public discussion. The mandate to be selective in the arguments we embrace is essential to successful daily living, as well as to the numerous frustrating dilemmas that will surely plague our future together. We have no realistic option to ignore problems when they arise. Ignore them for a while, and they will soon insist on grabbing our attention. So if we must eventually face them, we will need to develop as many critical thinkers as possible to sort and select optimal responses. *Asking the Right Questions* can be a strong tool for encouraging that development.

As a book ages, it becomes less and less the product of its original authors. The success of *Asking the Right Questions: A Guide to Critical Thinking* is a tribute to the sound advice we have received from the many readers who thought we could do better next time around and who told us so. In fact, one of our biggest challenges has been to pick and choose from among the suggestions.

Always uppermost in our mind has been the desire to retain the primary attributes of *Asking the Right Questions*, while adjusting to new emphases in our own thought and the evolving needs of our readers. For instance, while we can always think of dozens of additions that would, we believe, enhance new editions of *Asking the Right Questions*, we want most of all to keep the book readable and short. We are willing to pay the price of omitting several things that would be apposite in a more weighty treatment of critical thinking because those who adopt or learn from *Asking the Right Questions* have been so assertive in applauding the crispness and cohesion of our approach. Individual readers who do not see their suggestions included will surely understand that writing for a general audience requires us to omit many valuable components that we would certainly include were we writing for a more specialized group of readers.

This new edition, like its predecessors, has been modified while retaining the basic framework of a simplified guide to critical thinking. This latest version has especially benefited from the critical eyes of numerous students who have studied from the book. The special features of this edition include the following:

1. Rewriting most practice passages and many illustrative examples because the team of students and teachers we consulted preferred the new illustrations. They found them more fresh and relevant to the experience of contemporary students.

2. Emphasizing that critical thinking is not primarily an effort to demonstrate what is faulty about the thinking of others. Instead, it is a process for improving the beliefs and decisions each of us must make, and

3. Expanding the companion Web site containing multiple, diverse practice opportunities in response to the needs of the increasing numbers of students and teachers who wish to have internet access to practice materials.

4. Highlighting the **values** of critical thinking to provide a stronger rationale for why critical thinking is essential for a thoughtful life.

Critical thinking is initially a process of reaction. Someone has strung together a conclusion and some reasons that allegedly make the case for the conclusion. Our task is to decide whether the argument is one we wish to make our own. So any reasoning provides raw material for critical-thinking practice.

However, we are all more interested in some arguments than others, for some reasoning seems to have a more significant effect on our lives. So if those learning critical thinking are to be highly engaged in the hours of practice needed to become proficient at critical thinking, we require sample arguments that especially appeal to the primary users of the book. We decided to place greater reliance on student feedback about their interest in particular practice opportunities. The result is substantial improvement in the content and variety of the practice passages.

The seventh edition stressed the importance of social skills that would encourage the use of critical thinking. We have kept this emphasis in the new edition, and we are supplementing it with persistent encouragement to frame critical thinking in a particular way. We learned this from our colleagues in Japan who found that Japanese students were not eager to criticize deficiencies in the reasoning of others. But once those same students viewed critical thinking as an avenue toward improved development of their own thinking, they fastened on critical thinking as a skill and habit. Our students are also reluctant to criticize reasoning because of the social effects of their criticisms. Their reluctance often disappears, however, when they begin to sense the positive effect of such criticisms on their own conscious reflection.

We worked especially hard for this edition to improve the Web site. It is organized by chapter and contains practice passages of varying size and complexity. In addition, learners also need to see arguments that are relatively strong. We want to highlight what is particularly strong about these arguments, to provide readers a model of what is possible when someone tries to reason well. We are attempting to include even more practice passages with feedback on the student Web site, as well as short self-graded objective quizzes for each chapter, and an expanded "Authors Answer Typical Student Questions" section. The Teachers' Web site will also be greatly expanded with more suggestions for student assignments and examples of high-quality student papers with comments explaining the basis for making that determination.

In the spirit of emphasizing the role of values in guiding careful thinking, this new edition takes every opportunity to highlight the values that unite those of us who hope to think critically. Were we not especially loyal to autonomy, reasonableness, curiosity, and commitment, we would not be as willing to do the hard work associated with critical thinking. This new edition focuses on making these assumptions transparent for learners.

The success of previous editions of this book is potent testimony to our collective curiosity about what to believe. Our minds are under assault by experts and scam artists alike. Sorting among all their claims about what to eat, do, and believe is an incredibly difficult responsibility. We know that we need all the help we can get to protect ourselves from the dangers implicit in nonsense. We want to think carefully before we make a belief our own.

From the start of this book's history, we have been motivated by a variety of personal experiences and observations. First, we have been dismayed by the degree to which students and citizens in general increasingly depend on "experts," textbook writers, teachers, lawyers, politicians, journalists, and TV commentators. As the complexity of the world seems to increase at an accelerating rate, there is a greater tendency to become passive absorbers of information, uncritically accepting what is seen and heard. We are concerned that too many of us are not actively making personal choices about what to accept and what to reject.

At the same time, each of us has little choice but to rely on experts on a regular basis. Life is far too complex for us to pretend that we can take care of all our decisions by simply relying on our own resources. So, if we must depend on experts, how do we select from among the crowd of experts—each telling us he or she knows best? Critical thinking can help answer that question. It provides a set of filters that expert opinion needs to get through before you rely on it. In other words, all expert advice is not equally valuable. Critical thinking enables us to be more sensibly selective among experts.

Our experience in teaching critical-thinking skills to our students over a number of years has convinced us that when individuals with diverse abilities are taught these skills in a simplified format, they can learn to apply them successfully. In the process, they develop greater confidence in their ability to make rational choices about social issues, even those with which they have formerly had little experience.

Thus, we have written a text that does a number of things that other books have failed to do. This text develops an integrated series of question-asking skills that can be applied widely. These skills are discussed in an informal style. (We have written to a general audience, not to any specialized group.)

The development of *Asking the Right Questions* has leaned heavily on our joint experience of 65 years as teachers of critical thinking. Our ideas have evolved in response to numerous classroom experiences with students at many different levels, from freshman to Ph.D. students.

These experiences have taught us certain emphases that are particularly effective in learning critical thinking. For instance, we provide many opportunities for the readers to apply their skills and to receive immediate feedback following the practice application. The book is replete with examples of writing devoted to controversial contemporary topics. The breadth of topics introduces the average reader to numerous controversies with which he may have little familiarity. The book is coherently organized, in that critical questions are discussed sequentially as the reader progresses from understanding to evaluating.

One feature that deserves to be highlighted is the applicability of *Asking the Right Questions* to numerous life experiences extending far beyond the classroom. The habits and attitudes associated with critical thinking are transferable to consumer, medical, legal, and general ethical choices. When our surgeon says surgery is needed, it can be life sustaining to seek answers to the critical questions encouraged in *Asking the Right Questions.*

Who would find *Asking the Right Questions* especially beneficial? Because of our teaching experiences with readers representing many different levels of ability, we have difficulty envisioning any academic course or program for which this book would not be useful. In fact, the first seven editions have been used in law, English, pharmacy, philosophy, education, psychology, sociology, religion, and social science courses, as well as in numerous high-school classrooms.

A few uses for the book seem especially appropriate. Teachers in general education programs may want to begin their courses by assigning it as a coherent response to their students' requests to explain what is expected of them. English courses that emphasize expository writing could use this text both as a format for evaluating arguments prior to constructing an essay and as a checklist of problems that the writer should attempt to avoid as she writes. The book is especially functional in courses for training prospective teachers and graduate assistants because it makes explicit much that teachers will want to encourage in their students. Especially important, it encourages an orderly approach to evaluative thinking. While critical thinking need not be formulaic in any fashion, learning something as cognitively demanding as critical thinking is facilitated by an integrated approach. Supplementing their current content with our step-by-step description of the process of critical reading and thinking may enrich courses in study-skill development. The text can also be used as the central focus of courses designed specifically to teach critical reading and thinking skills.

While *Asking the Right Questions* stems primarily from our classroom experiences, it is written so that it can guide the reading and listening habits of almost everyone. The skills that it seeks to develop are those that any critical reader needs to serve as a basis for rational decisions. The critical questions stressed in the book can enhance anyone's reasoning, regardless of the extent of his or her formal education.

This eighth edition owes special debts to many people. We wish to acknowledge the valuable advice of the following Prentice Hall reviewers: Patricia Allen, MassBay Community College; Dr. Alan Baragona, Virginia Military Institute; Lisa Barnes, Delware Country Community College; Thomas J. Martin, University of North Carolina; Charlotte P. Brian, McNeece Imperial Valley College; Michael A. Schwartz, University of Florida; Brian Allan, Wooters Metropolitan Community College; Thomas Young, Mansfield University.

While our students are always a major source of suggested improvements, a few distinguished themselves in that regard. The seventh edition benefited from the valuable assistance of Dan Tagliarina, Heather Tewksbury, and Steve Weigand.

M. Neil Browne
Stuart M. Keeley

CHAPTER

1

The Benefit of Asking the Right Questions

Introduction

Any of us who enjoy movies are curious about the content of the latest films. Should we go see them now, wait for them to show up at our preferred rental location, or avoid them altogether? Lots of film experts are available to advise us. But which of their opinions should we follow? Opinions are cheap; anyone can have one of those. But which film expert possesses the kind of knowledge that gives us an opinion on which we can rely?

The authors of this book are film fanatics, but we both want to be selective in what we see. While we are fascinated by film as a medium, there are many films that we do not wish to see. Deciding which those are is hard work. To make the task easier, we often use one of our favorite web sites, http://www.rottentomatoes.com.

However, one of the most obvious things one learns when reading dozens of reviews of a particular film is the certainty that human judgment will not be identical. Pick any movie you wish; check the reviews. Regardless of how many reviewers hated the movie, some reviewer somewhere will string together a positive review. Similarly, pick the most popular movie in history; go to the reviews. What do you find? Some expert thought it was a dog.

This experience is a metaphor for much of life. Doctors, legislators, architects, plumbers, and detectives all disagree among themselves about the proper course of action in particular circumstances. How are we consumers of opinions to respond? The book you are about to read contains the best answer we know. You need to build skills and attitudes that will enable you to decide for yourself which opinions to make your own.

As a thoughtful person you must make a choice about how you will react to what you see and hear. One alternative is to just accept whatever you encounter; doing so automatically results in your making someone else's opinion your own. A more active alternative consists of asking questions in an effort to reach a personal decision about the worth of what you have experienced. This book is written for those who prefer the second alternative.

Critical Thinking to the Rescue

Listening and reading critically—that is, reacting with systematic evaluation to what you have heard and read—requires a set of skills and attitudes. These skills and attitudes are built around a series of related critical questions. While we will learn them one by one, our goal is to be able to use them together to identify the best decision available.

We could have expressed them as a list of things you should do, but a system of questions is more consistent with the spirit of curiosity, wonder, and intellectual adventure essential to critical thinking. Thinking carefully is always an unfinished project, a story looking for an ending that will never arrive. Critical questions provide a stimulus and direction for critical thinking; they move us forward toward a continual, ongoing search for better opinions, decisions, or judgments.

Consequently, **critical thinking**, as we will use the term, refers to the following:

1. awareness of a set of interrelated critical questions;
2. ability to ask and answer critical questions at appropriate times; and the
3. desire to actively use the critical questions.

The goal of this book is to encourage you in all three of these dimensions.

Questions require the person being asked the question to act in response. By our questions, we are saying to the person: I am curious; I want to know more; help me. This request shows respect for the other person. The questions exist to inform and provide direction for all who hear them. In that respect, critical thinking begins with the desire to improve what we think. The point of your questions is that you need help to have a deeper understanding or appreciation of what is being said.

The critical questions will be shared with you one question at a time. As a package, they will be useful whenever you choose to react to what you are hearing or reading. They are also useful in improving your own writing and speaking because they will assist you when you:

1. react critically to an essay or to evidence presented in a textbook, a periodical, or on a Web site;

2. judge the quality of a lecture or speech;

3. form an argument;

4. write an essay based on a reading assignment; or

5. participate in class.

> **Attention:**   Critical thinking consists of an awareness of a set of interrelated critical questions, plus the ability and willingness to ask and answer them at appropriate times.

As a citizen and consumer, you should find them especially helpful in shaping your voting behavior and your purchasing decisions, as well as in improving your self-confidence by increasing your sense of intellectual independence.

The Sponge and Panning for Gold: Alternative Thinking Styles

One approach to thinking is similar to the way in which a sponge reacts to water: by absorbing. This commonly used approach has some clear advantages.

First, the more information you absorb about the world, the more capable you are of understanding its complexities. Knowledge you have acquired provides a foundation for more complicated thinking later.

A second advantage of the sponge approach is that it is relatively passive. Rather than requiring strenuous mental effort, it tends to be rather quick and easy, especially when the material is presented in a clear and interesting fashion. The primary mental effort involves concentration and memory.

While absorbing information provides a productive start toward becoming a thoughtful person, the sponge approach has a serious disadvantage: It provides no method for deciding which information and opinions to believe and which to reject. If a reader relied on the sponge approach all the time, he would believe whatever he read last. The idea of being the mental puppet of whomever one happens to encounter is horrible imagery for a person and a community. Decisions become accidents of association, instead of reflective judgments.

We think you would rather choose for yourself what to absorb and what to ignore. To make this choice, you must read with a special attitude—a question-asking attitude. Such a thinking style requires active participation. The writer is trying to speak to you, and you should try to talk back to him, even though he is not present.

We call this interactive approach the panning-for-gold style of thinking. The process of panning for gold provides a model for active readers and listeners as they try to determine the worth of what they read and hear. The task is challenging and sometimes tedious, but the reward can be tremendous. To distinguish the gold from the gravel in a conversation requires you to ask frequent questions and to reflect on the answers.

The sponge approach emphasizes knowledge acquisition; the panning-for-gold approach stresses active interaction with knowledge as it is being acquired. Thus, the two approaches complement each other. To pan for intellectual gold, there must be something in your pan to evaluate. In addition, to evaluate arguments, we must possess knowledge, dependable opinions.

Let us examine more closely how the two approaches lead to different behavior. What does the individual who takes the sponge approach do when he reads material? He reads sentences carefully, trying to remember as much as he can. He may underline or highlight key words and sentences. He may take notes summarizing the major topics and major points. He checks his underlining or notes to be sure that he is not forgetting anything important. His mission is to find and understand what the author has to say. He memorizes the reasoning, but doesn't evaluate it.

What does the reader who takes the panning-for-gold approach do? Like the person using the sponge approach, he approaches his reading with the hope that he will acquire new knowledge. There the similarity ends. The panning-for-gold approach requires that the reader asks himself a number of questions designed to uncover the best available decisions or beliefs.

Exhibit 1.1   MENTAL CHECK: *Am I Panning for Gold?*

√   Did I ask "why" someone wants me to believe something?

√   Did I take notes as I thought about potential problems with what was being said?

√   Did I evaluate what was being said?

√   Did I form my own conclusion about the topic?

The reader who uses the panning-for-gold approach frequently questions why the author makes various claims. He writes notes to himself in the margins indicating problems with the reasoning. He continually interacts with the material. His intent is to critically evaluate the material and formulate personal conclusions based on the evaluation.

An Example of the Panning-for-Gold Approach

A major enduring issue in American society concerns what kind of gun control laws we need. Let's look at one position on this issue. Try to decide whether the argument is convincing.

> Arguments for banning guns are mostly myths, and what we need now is not more laws, but more law enforcement. One myth is that most murderers are ordinary, law-abiding citizens who kill a relative or acquaintance in a moment of anger only because a gun is available. In fact, every study of homicide shows the overwhelming majority of murderers are career criminals, people with lifelong histories of violence. The typical murderer has a prior criminal history averaging at least six years, with four major felony arrests.
>
> Another myth is that gun owners are ignorant rednecks given to senseless violence. However, studies consistently show that, on the average, gun owners are better educated and have more prestigious jobs than non-owners. To judge by their applications for permits to carry guns at all times, the following are (or were) gun owners: Eleanor Roosevelt, Joan Rivers, Donald Trump, and David Rockefeller.
>
> A further myth is that guns are not useful for self-defense. On the contrary! Every study has shown that handguns are used more often in repelling crimes than in committing them. While handguns are used in about 581,000 crimes yearly, they are used to repel about 645,000 crimes.
>
> Even if gun laws do potentially reduce gun-related crime, the present laws are all that are needed if they are enforced. What good would stronger laws do when the courts have demonstrated that they will not enforce them?

If you apply the sponge approach to the passage, you probably will try to remember the reasons that we don't need further controls on guns. If so, you will have absorbed some knowledge. However, how convinced should you be by the above reasons? You can't evaluate them until you have applied the panning-for-gold approach to the passage—that is, until you have asked the right questions.

By asking the right questions, you would discover a number of possible weaknesses in the communicator's arguments. For instance, you might be concerned about all of the following:

1. What does the author mean by "overwhelming majority" or by "typical murderer"? Is the minority still a substantial number of murderers who kill relatives in a moment of anger?

2. What does "gun owners" mean? Are they the ones who buy the kind of guns that gun control advocates are trying to ban?

3. How adequate were the cited research studies? Were the samples sufficiently large, random, and diverse?

4. Has the author lied with statistics by impressing us with large, rather precise numbers, like 581,000 and 645,000? What is the basis for these numbers? Can we rely on them?

5. What possible benefits of gun control are not mentioned? Have important studies that disagree with the author's position been omitted?

6. Is it legitimate to assume that because some famous people own guns, then owning guns is desirable? Do these people have special expertise concerning the pros and cons of gun ownership?

7. How many people are killed each year by handguns who would not have been killed were such guns not available?

8. Why did the person writing the essay fail to explain how we could encourage better enforcement of existing gun control laws to demonstrate his sensitivity to the harm that guns sometimes facilitate?

If you would enjoy asking these kinds of questions, this book is especially for you. Its primary purpose is to help you know when and how to ask questions that will enable you to decide what to believe.

The most important characteristic of the panning-for-gold approach is interactive involvement—a dialogue between the writer and the reader, or the speaker and the listener.

Clearly, there are times when the sponge approach is appropriate. Most of you have used it regularly and have acquired some level of success with it. It is much less likely that you are in the habit of employing the panning-for-gold approach—in part, simply because you have not had the appropriate training and practice. This book will not only help you ask the right questions, but will also provide frequent opportunities for practicing their use.

Panning for Gold: Asking Critical Questions

It would be relaxing if what other people were really saying were always obvious, if all their essential thoughts were clearly labeled for us, if the writer or speaker never made an error in her reasoning, and if all knowledgeable people agreed about answers to important questions. If this were the case, we could read and listen passively and let others do our thinking for us.

However, the true state of affairs is quite the opposite. A person's reasoning is often not obvious. Important elements are often missing. Many of the elements that are present are unclear. Consequently, you need critical reading and listening skills to help you determine what makes sense and distinguish this clear thinking from the sloppy thinking that characterizes much of what you will encounter.

The inadequacies in what someone says will not always leap out at you. You must be an *active* reader and listener. You can do this by *asking questions*. The best search strategy is a critical-questioning strategy. A powerful advantage of these questions is that they permit you to ask searching questions even when you know very little about the topic being discussed. For example, you do not need to be an expert on childcare to ask critical questions about the adequacy of day-care centers.

The Myth of the "Right Answer"

Our ability to find definite answers to questions often depends on the type of question that puzzles us. Scientific questions about the physical world are the most likely to have answers that reasonable people will accept, because the physical world is in certain ways more dependable or predictable than the social world. While the precise distance to the moon or the age of a newly discovered bone from an ancient civilization may not be absolutely certain, agreement about the dimensions of our physical environment is widespread. Thus, in the physical sciences, we frequently can arrive at "the right answer."

Questions about human behavior are different. The causes of human behavior are so complex that we frequently cannot do much more than form intelligent guesses about why or when certain behavior will occur. In addition, because many of us care a great deal about explanations and descriptions of human behavior, we prefer that explanations or descriptions of the rate of abortion, the frequency of unemployment, or the causes of child abuse be consistent with what we want to believe. Hence, we bring our preferences to any discussion of those issues and resist arguments that are inconsistent with them.

Because human behavior is so controversial and complex, the best answers that we can find for many questions about our behavior will be probabilistic in nature. Even if we were aware of every bit of evidence about the effects of exercise on our mental health, we could still not expect certainty about those effects. We still need to commit to a particular course of action to prevent our becoming a "hollow man" or a "nowhere woman." But once we acknowledge that our commitments are based on probability and not certainty, we will be much more open to the reasoning of those who are trying to persuade us to change our minds. After all, we may well be wrong about some of our beliefs.

Regardless of the type of questions being asked, the issues that require your closest scrutiny are usually those about which "reasonable people" disagree. In fact, many issues are interesting exactly because there is strong disagreement about how to resolve them. Any controversy involves more than one position. Several positions may be supported with good reasons. There will seldom be a position on a social controversy about which you will be able to say, "This is clearly the right position on the issue." If such certainty were possible, reasonable people would not be debating the issue. Our focus in this book will be on such social controversies.

Even though you will not necessarily arrive at the "right answer" to social controversies, this book is designed to give you the skills to develop your best and most reasonable answer, given the nature of the problem and the available information. Decisions usually must be made in the face of uncertainty. Often we will not have the time or the ability to discover many of the important facts about a decision we must make. For example, it is simply unwise to ask all the right questions when someone you love is complaining of sharp chest pains and wants you to transport him to the emergency room.

Thinking and Feeling

When you first encounter a conclusion, you do so with a history. You have learned to care about certain things, to support particular interests, and to discount claims of a particular type. So you always start to think critically in the midst of existing opinions. You have emotional commitments to these existing opinions. They are *your* opinions, and you quite understandably feel protective of them.

This point deserves special emphasis. We bring lots of personal baggage to every decision we make—experiences, dreams, values, training, and cultural habits.

However, if you are to grow, you need to recognize these feelings, and, as much as you are able, put them on a shelf for a bit. Only that effort will enable you to listen carefully when others offer arguments that threaten or violate your current beliefs. This openness is important because many of our own positions on issues are not especially reasonable ones; they are opinions given to us by others, and over many years we develop emotional attachments to them. Indeed, we frequently believe that we are being personally attacked when someone presents a conclusion contrary to our own. The danger of being emotionally involved in an issue is that you may fail to consider potential good reasons for other positions—reasons that might be sufficient to change your mind on the issue if only you would listen to them.

Remember: Emotional involvement should not be the primary basis for accepting or rejecting a position. Ideally, emotional involvement should be most intense *after* reasoning has occurred. Thus, when you read, try to avoid letting emotional involvement cut you off from the reasoning of those with whom you initially disagree. A successful active learner is one who is willing to change his mind. If you are ever to change your mind, you must be as open as possible to ideas that strike you as weird or dangerous when you first encounter them.

Critical thinkers, however, are not machines. They care greatly about many issues. The depth of that concern can be seen in their willingness to do all the hard mental work associated with critical thinking. But any passion felt by critical thinkers is moderated by the recognition that their current beliefs are open to revision.

The Efficiency of Asking the Question, "Who Cares?"

Asking good questions is difficult but rewarding work. Some controversies will be much more important to you than others. When the consequences of a controversy for you and your community are minimal, you will want to spend less time and energy thinking critically about it than about more important controversies. For example, it makes sense to critically evaluate arguments for and against the protection of endangered species, because different positions on this issue lead to important consequences for society. It makes less sense to devote energy to evaluating whether blue is the favorite color of most corporate executives.

Your time is valuable. Before taking the time to critically evaluate an issue, ask the question, "Who cares?"

Weak-Sense and Strong-Sense Critical Thinking

Previous sections mentioned that you already have opinions about many personal and social issues. You are willing right now to take a position on such questions as: Should prostitution be legalized? Is alcoholism a disease or willful misconduct? Was George Bush a successful president? You bring these initial opinions to what you hear and read.

Critical thinking can be used to either (1) defend *or* (2) evaluate and revise your initial beliefs. Professor Richard Paul's distinction between weak-sense and strong-sense critical thinking helps us appreciate these two antagonistic uses of critical thinking.

> **Attention:** Weak-sense critical thinking is the use of critical thinking to defend your current beliefs. Strong-sense critical thinking is the use of the same skills to evaluate all claims and beliefs, especially your own.

If you approach critical thinking as a method for defending your initial beliefs or those you are paid to have, you are engaged in *weak-sense critical thinking*. Why is it weak? To use critical-thinking skills in this manner is to be unconcerned with moving toward truth or virtue. The purpose of weak-sense critical thinking is to resist and annihilate opinions and reasoning different from yours. To see domination and victory over those who disagree with you as the objective of critical thinking is to ruin the potentially humane and progressive aspects of critical thinking.

In contrast, *strong-sense critical thinking* requires us to apply the critical questions to all claims, including our own. By forcing ourselves to look critically at our initial beliefs, we help protect against self-deception and conformity. It is easy to just stick with current beliefs, particularly when many people share them. But when we take this easy road, we run the strong risk of making mistakes we could otherwise avoid.

Strong-sense critical thinking does not necessarily force us to give up our initial beliefs. It can provide a basis for strengthening them because critical examination of those beliefs will sometimes reinforce our original commitment to them. A long time ago, John Stuart Mill warned us of the emptiness of a set of opinions accumulated without the help of strong-sense critical thinking:

> He who knows only his side of the case knows little of that. His reasons may have been good, and no one may have been able to refute them. But if he is equally unable to refute the reasons on the opposite side he has no ground for preferring either opinion.

To feel proud of a particular opinion, it should be one we have selected—selected from alternative opinions that we have understood and evaluated.

The Satisfaction of Using the Panning-for-Gold Approach

Doing is usually more fun than watching; doing well is more fun than simply doing. If you start using the interactive process taught in this book, you can feel the same sense of pride in your reading and listening that you normally get from successful participation in physical activities.

Critical thinkers find it satisfying to know when to say "no" to an idea or opinion and to know why that response is appropriate. If you regularly use the panning-for-gold approach, then anything that gets into your head will have been systematically examined first. When an idea or belief *does* pass the criteria developed here, it will make sense to agree with it—at least until new evidence appears.

Imagine how good you will feel if you know *why* you should ignore or accept a particular bit of advice. Frequently, those faced with an opinion different from their own respond by saying, "Oh, that's just your opinion." But the issue should not be whose opinion it is, but rather whether it is a good opinion. Armed with the critical questions discussed in this book, you can experience the satisfaction of knowing why certain advice is nonsense.

The sponge approach is often satisfying because it permits you to accumulate information. Though this approach is productive, there is much more gratification in being a participant in a meaningful dialogue with the writer or speaker. Reading and listening become much richer as you begin to see things that others may have missed. As you learn to select information and opinions systematically, you will probably desire to read more and more in a lifelong effort to decide which advice makes sense.

Trying Out New Answers

Although there is often no absolutely right answer, this book tries to encourage your search for better answers. Certainly, some answers are more accurate, appropriate, useful, or moral than are others. For you to want to do the hard work necessary to find better answers, you need substantial curiosity and even courage.

Courage is required because to keep looking for better answers we have to be willing to give up our current beliefs or positions. When we encounter a question, we probably already have an answer. Suppose someone says something to us about the appropriateness of behavior by abortion activists. In all probability, we already have an opinion about the matter. It often takes incredible courage to give up on an opinion we have held for some time after listening to someone else. As critical thinkers, we have to struggle to force ourselves to try out new answers. The interplay between our old answers and new ones provides a basis for our growth.

Effective Communication and Critical Thinking

Many of the skills you will learn, as you become a more critical thinker, will improve the quality of your writing and speaking. As you write and speak, it helps to be aware of the expectations careful thinkers will have. Because your objective is communication, many of the questions the thoughtful person will ask in evaluating your writing or speech should serve as guides for your own attempts to communicate well. Several of the critical questions that we urge you to ask highlight problems you will want to avoid as you write or speak.

While the emphasis in this book is on effective thinking, the link to competent communication is so direct that it will be a theme throughout. Wherever appropriate, we will mention how the skill being encouraged is an aid to improved communication.

The Importance of Practice

Learning new critical-thinking skills is a lot like learning new physical skills. You cannot learn simply by being told what to do or by watching others. You have to practice, and frequently the practice will be both rewarding and hard work. Our goal is to make your learning as simple as possible. However, acquiring the habit of critical thinking will initially take a lot of practice.

The practice exercises and sample responses at the end of each chapter are an important part of this text. Try to do the exercises and, only then, compare your answers with ours. Our answers are not necessarily the only correct ones, but they provide illustrations of how to apply the question-asking skills. We intentionally failed to provide sample answers for the third passage at the end of each chapter. Our objective is to give you the opportunity to struggle with the answer using your knowledge of the chapter you have just studied. We want you to feel the accomplishment of no longer necessarily needing us to guide you.

The Right Questions

To give you an initial sense of the skills that *Asking the Right Questions* will help you acquire, we will list the critical questions for you here. By the end of the book, you should know when and how to ask these questions productively:

1. What are the issues and the conclusions?
2. What are the reasons?
3. Which words or phrases are ambiguous?
4. What are the value conflicts and assumptions?
5. What are the descriptive assumptions?
6. Are there any fallacies in the reasoning?
7. How good is the evidence?
8. Are there rival causes?
9. Are the statistics deceptive?
10. What significant information is omitted?
11. What reasonable conclusions are possible?

WHAT ARE THE ISSUE AND THE CONCLUSION?

Before we evaluate someone's reasoning, we must first find it. Doing so sounds simple; it isn't. To get started as a critical thinker, you must practice the identification of the issue and the conclusion.

issue
Cell phone
use

concl.

Police the
use

Cell phones are becoming a large part of today's society bringing with than benefits and drawbacks. They are beneficial for those with tight schedules and in case of emergencies. Cell phones can also come in handy for parents to check up on their children. Even though cell phones do carry benefits, the drawbacks are in their inappropriate use. When a cell phone rings or owners talk on them during a lecture or a concert, a major disruption in the concentration of others is inevitable. Even though there are suggestions in polite society to leave them off, perhaps we need stronger penalties associated with abuse of the growing population of cell phones.

The person who wrote this assessment of cell phones very much wants you to believe something. But what is that something and why are we supposed to believe any such thing?

In general, those who create Web pages, editorials, books, magazine articles, or speeches are trying to change your perceptions or beliefs. For you to form a reasonable reaction to their persuasive effort, you must first identify the controversy or *issue* as well as the thesis or conclusion being pushed onto you. (Someone's *conclusion* is her intended message to you. Its purpose is to shape your beliefs and/or behavior.) Otherwise, you will be reacting to a distorted version of the attempted communication.

When we read or listen, it is so easy to ignore what was said in the previous paragraph. We often react to the images, dramatic illustrations, or tone of what was said instead of the reasoning that was intended by the person communicating with us. Each time we fail to react to the reasoning, human conversation has experienced a defeat. We are not connecting as the person who wrote or spoke to us intended. So, getting straight about the person's conclusion and issue is an essential first step in effective human interaction.

When you have completed this chapter, you should be able to answer the first of our critical questions successfully:

 Critical Question: ***What are the issue and the conclusion?***

Attention: An issue is a question or controversy responsible for the conversation or discussion. It is the stimulus for what is being said.

Kinds of Issues

It will be helpful at this point to identify two kinds of issues you will typically encounter. The following questions illustrate one of these:

Do families who own pets have fewer arguments with one another?

What causes high blood pressure?

Who made the decision to increase our sales taxes?

How much will college cost in the year 2010?

All these questions have one thing in common. They demand answers attempting to describe the way the world is, was, or is going to be. For example, answers to the first two questions might be, "In general, families with pets have fewer arguments with one another," and "Poor dietary habits cause high blood pressure."

Such issues are *descriptive issues.* They are commonly found in textbooks, magazines, the Internet, and television. Such issues reflect our curiosity about patterns or order in the world. Note the boldfaced words that begin each question above; when questions begin with these words, they will probably be descriptive questions.

Attention: Descriptive issues are those that raise questions about the accuracy of descriptions of the past, present, or future.

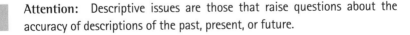

Now let's look at examples of a second kind of question:

Should capital punishment be abolished?

What ought to be done about social security?

Must we outlaw SUVs or face increasing rates of asthma?

All of these questions demand answers suggesting the way the world *ought to be*. For example, answers to the first two questions might be, "Capital punishment *should be* abolished," and "We *ought* to increase social security benefits."

These issues are ethical, or moral, issues; they raise questions about what is right or wrong, desirable or undesirable, good or bad. They demand prescriptive answers. Thus, we will refer to these issues as *prescriptive issues*. Social controversies are often prescriptive issues.

We have somewhat oversimplified. Sometimes it will be difficult to decide what kind of issue is being discussed. It will be useful to keep these distinctions in mind, however, because the kinds of critical evaluations you eventually make will differ depending on the kind of issue to which you are responding.

> **Attention:**   Prescriptive issues are those that raise questions about what we should do or what is right or wrong, good or bad.

Searching for the Issue

How does one go about determining the basic question or issue? Sometimes it is very simple: The writer or speaker will tell you what it is. Alternatively, the issue may be identified in the body of the text, usually right at the beginning, or it may even be found in the title. When the issue is explicitly stated, it will be indicated by phrases such as the following:

The question I am raising is: Why must we have speed limits on our highways?

Lowering the legal drinking age: *Is it the right thing to do?*

Should sex education be taught in the schools?

Unfortunately, the question is not always explicitly stated and instead must be inferred from other clues in the communication. For example, many writers or speakers are reacting to some current event that concerns them, such as a series of violent acts in schools. Asking "What is the author reacting to?" will often suggest the central issue of a communication. Another good clue is knowledge of the author's background, such as organizations to which she belongs. So check for background information about the author as you try to determine the issue.

When you are identifying the issue, try to resist the idea that there is one and only one correct way to state the issue. Once you have found a question that the entire essay or speech is addressing, and you can show the link between that question and the essay or speech, *you have found the issue.* Just make certain that what you are calling an issue meets the definitional criteria for that idea.

The surest way to detect an issue when it is not explicitly stated, however, is to locate the conclusion. In many cases, the conclusion must be found before you can identify the issue. Thus, in such cases, the first step in critical evaluation is to find the conclusion—a frequently difficult step.

We cannot critically evaluate until we find the conclusion!

Let's see how we go about looking for that very important structural element.

> **Attention:** A conclusion is the message that the speaker or writer wishes you to accept.

Searching for the Author's or Speaker's Conclusion

To identify the conclusion, the critical thinker must ask, "What is the writer or speaker trying to prove?" or "What is the communicator's main point?" The answer to either of these questions will be the conclusion. Any answer to the question provided by the speaker or writer will be the conclusion.

In searching for a conclusion, you will be looking for a statement or set of statements that the writer or speaker wants you to believe. She wants you to believe the conclusion on the basis of her other statements. In short, the basic structure of persuasive communication or argument is: *This* because of *that. This* refers to the conclusion; *that* refers to the support for the conclusion. This structure represents the process of *inference.*

Conclusions are *inferred;* they are derived from reasoning. Conclusions are ideas that require other ideas to support them. Thus, whenever someone claims something is true or ought to be done and provides no statements to support her claim, that claim is not a conclusion because no one has offered any basis for belief. In contrast, unsupported claims are what we refer to as *mere* opinions.

The last paragraph says a lot. It would be a good idea for you to read it again. Understanding the nature of a conclusion is an essential step toward critical reading and listening. Let's look closely at a conclusion and at the inference process. Here is a brief paragraph; see whether you can identify the conclusion, then the statements that support it.

> Factory farming should not be legal. There are other more natural ways to produce needed food supply.

"Factory farming should not be legal." This is the author's answer to the question: should factory farming be legalized? It is her conclusion. The author supports this belief with another: "There are other more natural ways to produce needed food supply."

Do you see why the supporting belief is not a conclusion? It is not the conclusion because it is used to prove something else. *Remember.* To believe one statement (the conclusion) because you think it is well supported by *other* beliefs is to make an inference. When people engage in this process, they are reasoning; the conclusion is the outcome of this reasoning.

Sometimes, communicators will not make their conclusions explicit; in such cases you will have to infer the conclusion from what you believe the author is trying to prove by the set of ideas she has presented.

USING THIS CRITICAL QUESTION

Once you have found the conclusion, use it as the focus of your evaluation. It is the destination that the writer or speaker wants you to choose. Your ongoing concern is: Should I accept that conclusion on the basis of what is supporting the claim?

Clues to Discovery: How to Find the Conclusion

There are a number of clues to help you identify the conclusion.

CLUE No. 1: **Ask what the issue is.** Because a conclusion is always a response to an issue, it will help you find the conclusion if you know the issue. We discussed earlier how to identify the issue. First, look at the title. Next, look at the opening paragraphs. If this technique does not help, skimming several pages may be necessary.

Clue No. 2: **Look for indicator words.** The conclusion will frequently be preceded by indicator words that announce a conclusion is coming. When you see these indicator words, take note of them. They tell you that a conclusion may follow. A list of such indicator words follows:

consequently	suggests that
hence	therefore
points	to the conclusion that
thus	the point I'm trying to make is
it follows that	it is highly probable that
shows that	proves that
indicates that	the truth of the matter is

Read the following passage; then identify and highlight the indicator words. By doing so, you will have identified the statements containing the conclusion.

> Because of the wording of the Constitution, it follows that prayer should not be allowed in public schools. When the schools favor any particular religion, they are hampering the freedom of those who embrace a different religion. The idea of freedom of religion is what the country was founded on.

You should have highlighted the following phrase: *it follows*. The conclusion follows these words.

Unfortunately, many written and spoken communications do not introduce the conclusion with indicator words. However, when *you* write, you should draw attention to your thesis with indicator words. Those words act as a neon sign, drawing attention to the point you want the reader to accept.

Clue No. 3: **Look in likely locations.** Conclusions tend to occupy certain locations. The first two places to look are at the beginning and at the end. Many writers begin with a statement of purpose, containing what they are trying to prove. Others summarize their conclusions at the end. If you are reading a long, complex passage and are having difficulty seeing where it is going, skip ahead to the end.

Clue No. 4: **Remember what a conclusion is not.** Conclusions will not be any of the following:

- examples
- statistics
- definitions
- background information
- evidence

Clue No. 5: **Check the context of the communication and the author's background.** Often writers, speakers, or Internet sites take predictable positions on issues. Knowing probable biases of the source and the background of authors can be especially valuable clues when the conclusion is not explicit. Be especially alert to information about organizations with which writers or speakers may be associated.

Clue No. 6: **Ask the question, "and therefore?"** Because conclusions are often implied, ask for the identity of the "and therefore" element. Ask, "Does the author want us to draw an implied conclusion from the information communicated?" Conclusions like "candidate X will be soft on crime" are often left for the reader or viewer to infer from the limited information presented in a political ad.

Critical Thinking and Your Own Writing and Speaking

Because readers of your writing will be looking for *your* thesis or conclusion, help them by giving it the clarity it deserves. It is the central message you want to deliver. Emphasize it; leave no doubt about what it actually is. Making your conclusion easily identifiable not only makes a reader's task easier, it also may improve the logic of your writing. An effective way to emphasize the conclusion is to insert it at the beginning or end of your essay and precede it with an indicator word.

In addition, take a close look at your conclusion to make certain that it is a direct response to the issue you intended to address. For example, suppose the issue you are attempting to address is: Will owning a pet increase how long we live? If your conclusion is: "yes, it will increase our life span by an average of 15 years," there is a match between issue and conclusion. But were your conclusion, instead, that pets bring joy to the lives of everyone who owns them, your reasoning is confused. The latter conclusion is responding to a different issue, namely, do pets bring joy to our lives?

Practice Exercises

Critical Question: **What are the issue and the conclusion?**

In the following passages, locate the issue and conclusion. As you search, be sure to look for indicator words.

Passage 1

Home schooling is a valid concept if the parent makes teaching a full time job, and has the insight, knowledge and patience to do so. However, the truth of the matter is that few parents who home school their child are capable of doing so.

Parents may choose to pull their student out of public schools for the wrong reasons. Sometimes, when children are a discipline problem, the parents will pull them out of school rather than tolerating the rules associated with the punishment. Such a motivation does not speak well for the probable results of the home schooling that follows. In addition, when there are no other adults to monitor what is going on at home, it is likely that if there is a case of abuse in the home that it will go unnoticed. Society needs to know whether these children are getting the education and treatment they deserve.

Passage 2

Television advertising agencies are very clever in the way that they construct ads. Often the ads are similar to the cartoons that the children enjoy. Children see these characters interacting with a certain product and associate their affection for the character with affection for the product. The companies do not want the children to perceive a difference between the shows they are watching and the advertisements. By using this strategy, these companies take advantage of the fact that children are often not able to discriminate between the cartoons and the ads and do not understand that these things offered come at a cost. Often the advertising is about sugary snacks or fatty foods, leading the children down a path to bad health. Advertising geared towards children should be regulated – just as there are regulations now about tobacco and alcohol ads targeted at children.

Passage 3

Should the public be shown actual courtroom trials on television? It seems as though the system can easily be corrupted by having cameras in the courtroom. Victims are hesitant enough when testifying in front of a small crowd, but their knowledge that every word is being sent to countless homes would increase the likelihood that they would simply refuse to testify. There is little to no assumed innocence for the accused when their trial is put on television. People do not watch court television because they are concerned about our country's ability to effectively carry out the proceedings of the judicial system; instead, they are looking for the drama in witness testimony: entertainment. Thus, leave the cameras out of the courtrooms, and let the public view sitcom drama based off of the legal system.

Sample Responses

Passage 1

The author states her conclusion in the second sentence of the passage. The conclusion is identified by the phrase, "the truth of the matter is". The author does not explicitly state the issue, but it can be inferred by the conclusion and the reasons. There are listed reasons in the second paragraph that suggest why some parents' motivation to home school their children would lend to an ineffective home schooling experience. This example is prescriptive because it asks what ought to be done.

ISSUE: *Should all parents be allowed to home school their children?*

CONCLUSION: *No, most parents are not capable of home schooling.*

Passage 2

There are no indicator words to point towards the conclusion, but a good place to look for the conclusion is either at the beginning or end of the excerpt. In this case, the very last statement is the conclusion, and you can tell it is the conclusion because it gives finality to the passage using the phrase "should be". This phrase also indicates that this is a prescriptive issue. It is not talking about the way things are or are not, but how they ought to be. The issue is assumed from the conclusion and from the preceding statements explaining why the author came to her conclusion.

ISSUE: *Should advertisements geared towards children be regulated?*

CONCLUSION: *Advertisements geared toward children should be regulated.*

CRITICAL QUESTION SUMMARY: WHY THIS QUESTION IS IMPORTANT

What Are the Issue and the Conclusion?

Before you can evaluate an author's argument, you must clearly identify the issue and conclusion. How can you evaluate an argument if you don't know exactly what the author is trying to persuade you to believe? Finding an author's main point is the first step in deciding whether you will accept or reject it.

CHAPTER

3

WHAT ARE THE REASONS?

Reasons provide answers for our human curiosity about why someone makes a particular decision or holds a particular opinion.

> Every class should conclude with student evaluations.
>
> A pig is smarter than a mule.
>
> Employers should be able to fire any employee who refuses to take a drug test.

Those three claims are each missing something. We may or may not agree with them, but in their current form they are neither weak nor strong. None of the claims contains an explanation or rationale for *why* we should agree. Thus, if we heard someone make one of those three assertions, we would be left hungry for more.

What is missing is the reason or reasons responsible for the claims. *Reasons* are beliefs, evidence, metaphors, analogies, and other statements offered to support or justify conclusions. They are the statements that together form the basis for creating the credibility of a conclusion. Chapter 2 gave you some guidelines for locating two very important parts of the structure of an argument—the issue and the conclusion. This chapter focuses on techniques for identifying the third essential element of an argument— the reasons.

When a writer has a conclusion she wants you to accept, she must present reasons to persuade you that she is right and to show you *why*.

It is the mark of a rational person to support her beliefs with adequate proof, especially when the beliefs are of a controversial nature. For example, when someone asserts that we should exclude inexperienced lawyers from representing those charged with felonies, this assertion should be met with the challenge, "Why do you say that?" You should raise this question whether you agree or disagree.

The person's reasons may be either strong or weak, but you will not know until you have asked the question and identified the reasons. If the answer is "because I think so," you should be dissatisfied with the argument, because the "reason" is a mere restatement of the conclusion. However, if the answer is evidence concerning serious mistakes made by inexperienced lawyers in felony cases, you will want to consider such evidence when you evaluate the conclusion. Remember: *You cannot determine the worth of a conclusion until you identify the reasons.*

Identifying reasons is a particularly important step in critical thinking. An opinion cannot be evaluated fairly unless we ask why it is held and get a satisfactory response. Focusing on reasons requires us to remain open to and tolerant of views that might differ from our own. If we reacted to conclusions rather than to reasoning, we would tend to stick to the conclusions we brought to the discussion or essay, and those conclusions that agree with our own would receive our rapid assent. If we are ever to re-examine our own opinions, we must remain curious, open to the reasons provided by those people with opinions that we do not yet share.

*Critical Question: **What are the reasons?***

Reasons + Conclusion = Argument

In ordinary conversation, an argument refers to a disagreement, a time when blood pressure soars. We will use the concept in a very different manner. An *argument* is a combination of two forms of statements: a conclusion and the reasons allegedly supporting it. The partnership between reasons and conclusion establishes a person's argument. It is something we provide because we care about how people live their lives and what they believe. Our continual improvement depends on someone's caring enough about us to offer us arguments and to evaluate the ones we make. Only then will we be able to develop as thoughtful people.

Sometimes, an argument will consist of a single reason and a conclusion; often, however, several reasons will be offered to support the conclusion.

So when we refer to someone's argument, we might be referring to a single reason and its related conclusion or to the entire group of reasons and the conclusion it is intended to substantiate.

> **Attention:** Reasons are explanations or rationales for why we should believe a particular conclusion.

As we use the terms, *argument* and *reasoning* mean the same thing—the use of one or more ideas to support another idea. Thus when a communication lacks reasons, it is neither an argument nor an example of reasoning. Consequently, only arguments and reasoning can be logically flawed. Because a reason *by itself* is an isolated idea, it cannot reflect a logical relationship.

Several characteristics of arguments grab our attention:

- They have intent. Those who provide them hope to convince us to believe certain things or act in certain ways. Consequently, they call for a reaction. We can imitate the sponge or the gold prospector, but we ordinarily must respond somehow.
- Their quality varies. Critical thinking is required to determine the extent of quality in an argument.
- They have two essential visible components—a conclusion and reasons. Failure to identify either component destroys the opportunity to evaluate the argument. We cannot evaluate what we cannot identify.

That last point deserves some repetition and explanation. There is little purpose in rushing critical thinking. In fact, the philosopher Wittgenstein suggests that when one bright person addresses another, each should first say "Wait!" Taking the time to locate arguments before we assess what we think was said is only fair to the person providing the argument.

Initiating the Questioning Process

The first step in identifying reasons is to approach the argument with a questioning attitude, and the first question you should ask is a *why* question. You have identified the conclusion; now you wish to know why the conclusion makes sense. If a statement does not answer the question, "Why does the writer or speaker believe that?" then it is not a reason. To function as a reason, a statement (or group of statements) must provide support for a conclusion.

Let us apply the questioning attitude to the following paragraph. First we will find the conclusion; then we will ask the appropriate *why* question. Remember your guidelines for finding the conclusion. (The indicator words for the conclusion have been italicized.)

> (1) Should metal detectors be in place at every public school? (2) Teachers were surveyed about their opinions. (3) Many indicated that they never know what to expect from their students and thought that metal detectors would be a safe solution to unexpected circumstances. (4) 57 percent of teachers agreed that metal detectors would help the school become a safer environment. (5) *Therefore*, public schools should install metal detectors for safety.

What follows "*Therefore*" answers the question raised in statement (1). Thus, the conclusion is statement (5) ". . . public schools should instate metal detectors for safety." *Highlight the conclusion!*

 Attention: An argument consists of a conclusion and the reasons that allegedly support it.

We then ask the question, "Why does the writer or speaker believe the conclusion?" The statements that answer that question are the reasons. In this particular case, the writer provides us with evidence as reasons. Statements (3) and (4) jointly provide the evidence; that is, together they provide support for the conclusion. Together they serve as the reason for the conclusion. Thus, we can paraphrase the reason as: A majority of surveyed teachers believe that metal detectors would help the school's level of safety.

Now, try to find the reasons in the following paragraph. Again, first find the conclusion, highlight it, and then ask the *why* question.

> (1) Genetic screening of embryos is morally wrong. (2) People do not have the right to terminate a potential life just because it might not be the right sex, or may have a defect of some kind. (3) It cannot be said that a person's quality of life is severely changed by birth defect, or that parents should get to choose the sex of their baby.

There is no obvious indicator word for the conclusion in the paragraph, but the author is against genetic screening of embryos. The conclusion is: "Genetic screening of embryos is morally wrong." Why does the author believe this? The major reason given is that "People do not have the right to decide to terminate a potential life based on a set of their preferred criteria." Sentence (3) provides additional support for this reason.

One of the best ways for you to determine whether you have discovered a reason is to try to play the role of the communicator. Put yourself in her position and ask yourself, "Why am I in favor of this conclusion that I am supporting?" Try to put into your own words how you believe the communicator would answer this question. If you can paraphrase the answer, you have probably discovered her reasons.

As you determine a communicator's reasoning structure, you should treat any idea that seems to be used to support her conclusion as a reason, even if you do not believe it provides support for the conclusion. At this stage of critical thinking, you are trying to identify the argument. Because you want to be fair to the person who made the argument, it makes good sense to use the principle of charity. If the writer or speaker believed she was providing support for the conclusion with some evidence or logic, then we should at least consider the reasoning. There will be plenty of time later to evaluate the reasoning carefully.

Words That Identify Reasons

As was the case with conclusions, there are certain words that will typically indicate that a reason will follow. *Remember:* The structure of reasoning is *this, because of that.* Thus, the word *because,* as well as words synonymous with and similar in function to it, will frequently signal the presence of reasons. A list of indicator words for reasons follows:

as a result of	for the reason that
because of the fact that	in view of
is supported by	because the evidence is

Kinds of Reasons

There are many different kinds of reasons, depending on the kind of issue. Many reasons will be statements that present evidence. By *evidence,* we mean specific information that someone uses to furnish "proof" for something she is trying to claim is true. Communicators appeal to many kinds of evidence to "prove their point." These include "the facts," research findings, examples from real life, statistics, appeals to experts and authorities, personal testimonials, metaphors, and analogies. Different kinds of evidence are more appropriate in some situations than in others, and you will find it helpful to develop rules for yourself for determining what kinds of evidence are appropriate on given occasions.

You will often want to ask, "What kind of evidence is needed to support this claim?" and then determine whether such evidence has been offered. You should know that there are no uniform "codes of evidence" applicable to all cases of serious reasoning. A more detailed treatment of evidence appears in Chapters 8–11.

When a speaker or writer is trying to support a descriptive conclusion, the answer to the *why* question will typically be evidence.

The following example provides a descriptive argument; try to find the author's reasons.

> (1) The number of people in the United States that are obese is growing quickly.
> (2) Studies indicate that over 25 percent of Americans are obese, not to mention the numbers of simply overweight Americans.

You should have identified the first statement as the conclusion. It is a descriptive statement about the large number of Americans who are obese. The rest of the paragraph presents the evidence—the reason for the conclusion. *Remember:* The conclusion itself will not be evidence; it will be a belief supported by evidence or by other beliefs.

In prescriptive arguments, reasons are typically either general, prescriptive statements or descriptive beliefs or principles. The use of these kinds of statements to support a conclusion in a prescriptive argument is illustrated in the following:

> (1) In today's society, there are all sorts of regulations on media, such as television ratings. (2) Do these ratings allow for people to make educated decisions about what they will or will not watch? (3) Do these ratings entice some people to watch a show even though they know they are not supposed to? (4) How many parents actually go by the television ratings to deter their children from watching a show? (5) More often than not, the television ratings do not prevent children from watching shows society believes that they are not mature enough to watch. (6) Television ratings are unenforceable guidelines. (7) If one believes in the censorship of media for minors, items such as the V-chip should be used for this pupose rather than the simple tagged rating at the top of the screen.

The conflict here is about whether television ratings are desirable. The author argues that if society really is concerned about what children are watching, then it should implement the use of items such as the V-chip, as stated in sentence (7). Let us look for sentences that answer the question, "Why does the author believe this conclusion?" First, note that no evidence is presented. Sentences (2) and (3) jointly form one reason, a descriptive belief: The television ratings are not significant enough to affect change, and they may even encourage some to watch more harmful shows than they would have otherwise watched. The warnings are vague and can leave people thinking that the show may not be that "bad." Sentences (4) and (5) add a second reason: The television ratings do not really affect the choice of television shows for either parents or children. Sentence (6) provides a third reason: Television ratings cannot be enforced. There is no officer on duty other than parents, and if they do not agree with the ratings or are not around, the ratings are useless. These last two reasons are general beliefs. If the argument were expanded by the author, the beliefs themselves might be supported by evidence in some form.

Keeping the Reasons and Conclusions Straight

Much reasoning is long and not very well organized. Sometimes a set of reasons will support one conclusion, and that conclusion will function as the main reason for another conclusion. Reasons may be supported by other reasons. In especially complicated arguments, it is frequently difficult to keep the structure straight in your mind as you attempt to critically evaluate what you have read. To overcome this problem, try to develop your own organizing procedure for keeping the reasons and conclusions separate and in a logical pattern.

We have mentioned a number of techniques for you to use in developing a clear picture of the reasoning structure. If some other technique works better for you, by all means use it. The important point is to keep the reasons and conclusions straight as you prepare to evaluate.

Clues for Identifying and Organizing the Reasoning of a Passage

1. Circle indicator words.
2. Underline the reasons and conclusion in different colors of ink, or highlight the conclusion and underline the reasons.
3. Label the reasons and conclusion in the margin.
4. After reading long passages, make a list of reasons at the end of the essay.

USING THIS CRITICAL QUESTION

Once you have found the reasons, you need to come back to them again and again as you read or listen further. Their quality is crucial to a strong argument. The conclusion depends on their merit. *Weak reasons create weak reasoning!*

Reasons First, Then Conclusions

The first chapter warned you about the danger of weak-sense critical thinking. A warning signal that can alert you to weak-sense critical thinking should go off when you notice that reasons seem to be created (on the spot, even) only because they defend a previously held opinion. When someone is eager to share an opinion as if it were a conclusion, but looks puzzled or angry when asked for reasons, weak-sense critical thinking is the probable culprit.

Certainly, you have a large set of initial beliefs, which act as initial conclusions when you encounter controversies. As your respect for the importance of reasons grows, you will frequently expect those conclusions to stand or crumble on the basis of their support. Your strongest conclusions follow your reflection about the reasons and what they mean.

Be your own censor in this regard. You must shake your own pan when looking for gold. Try to avoid "reverse logic" or "backward reasoning," whereby reasons are an afterthought, following the selection of your conclusion. Ideally, reasons are the tool by which conclusions are shaped and modified.

"Fresh" Reasons and Your Growth

We need to remind ourselves again and again how important it is to force ourselves to pay attention to "fresh" reasons, those that we have not previously considered. Critical thinkers are proud to be open to new forms of reasoning. Being fair to such reasons is tough, but rewarding. What makes this task so difficult is the power of our current opinions. They provide a starting point for our reaction to reasoning. We come to each conversation, essay, or lecture with a loyalty to the beliefs we already have. Thus, our existing beliefs can be an obstacle to our listening and learning. But at another level, we know there are thoughtful reasons that we have not yet encountered. For our personal growth, we have to give "fresh" reasons a real chance to speak to us.

Critical Thinking and Your Own Writing and Speaking

When you are writing or speaking, you will want to keep your audience fore-most in your plans. They need to be clear about what you conclude and why you are concluding it. Do not hide your conclusion and reasons; display them openly. Give the audience a clear opportunity to see what you intend. Thus, your task is to use words, sentences, paragraphs, and indicator words to illu-minate the logical relationships in your argument.

Practice Exercises

(?) *Critical Question:* **What are the reasons?**

First survey the passage and highlight its conclusion. Then ask the question, "Why?" and locate the reasons. Use indicator words to help. Keep the conclu-sions and the reasons separate. Try to paraphrase the reason; putting the rea-sons in your own words helps clarify their meaning and function.

Passage 1

Public swimming pools can be a health hazard. Many public pools are not able to obey the sanitation regulations and therefore allow for the contraction of water-borne bacteria. Studies have shown that only 60 percent of public pools are able to maintain the proper amount of chlorine in the water, allowing for those who use the pool to be infected. Many pool users have become ill after the use of a public swimming pool.

Passage 2

Schools all around the nation are forming community service programs. Should students be required to do community service? There are many drawbacks to requiring such service.

Students will not be able to understand the concept of charity and benevolence if it is something they have to do. Forced charity seems contradictory to the con-cept of charity. If this concept loses value for the students because the service was not a choice, they will then resent the idea of community service and not volun-teer to do so at a later time in life.

Furthermore, because this community service would be coerced, the students may not perform at a high level. They may feel they will do the bare minimum of what is required. The students may also be resentful or rude to the people they are helping, which would also hamper the progress of the community service.

As you can see, forced community service may not be the best programming choice for schools.

Passage 3

In high school men's basketball and men's football usually dominate the Friday night schedule. Should it be that way? These games are significant to the high school experience, but not at the cost of the other sports in the school. Just because it has been a tradition does not mean that the format has to remain that way.

It is easier for most parents and other fans to make it out to the game on Friday nights. Therefore, it is easier for them to come see the men's basketball or men's football games. What about the girl's basketball team, or the swim team? Their games should not always be stuck on weekday afternoons and evenings. Their families often are not able to make it out to see them because most are working during the afternoons. The students who play these "secondary" sports are not getting a fair share of the spotlight; the schedule should change to accommodate these other sports.

Sample Responses

Passage 1

ISSUE: *What makes public pools a health hazard?*

CONCLUSION: *Inadequate sanitation.*

REASONS: 1. *Sixty percent of public pools are not able to maintain proper chlorination levels.*
            2. *Many people have gotten sick after using public pools.*

Recall that we are looking for the support system for the conclusion. We ask ourselves: Why does this person claim that sanitation is causing a health hazard in pools? The conclusion is justified by two research findings; these findings constitute the reasons. An indicator word for the first reason is "studies have shown."

Passage 2

ISSUE: *Should schools require community service?*

CONCLUSION: *No, schools should not require community service.*

REASONS: 1. *Forced charity makes little sense.*

(SUPPORTING REASONS)

a.   *Required community service is a self-contradiction.*

> b. *Students will resent the idea of community service and choose not to do so later in life.*
> c. *Students will not perform at a high level.*
>> 1. *The students will only do the bare minimum, not what would most benefit the recipient.*
>> 2. *Students may be rude to those they are helping.*

Why are we told that schools should not require community service? The answer to that question will be the author's reasons. The first reason is supported by a collection of examples and claims, all showing us that forced community service is a contradiction. *Furthermore* is the indicator word calling our attention to the second reason.

CRITICAL QUESTION SUMMARY: WHY THIS QUESTION IS IMPORTANT

What Are the Reasons?

Once you have identified the issue and conclusion, you need to understand *why* an author has come to a certain conclusion. Reasons are the *why.* If the author provides good reasons, you might be persuaded to accept her conclusion. However, right now, we are simply concerned with identifying the reasons. Identifying the reasons is the next step in deciding whether you should accept or reject the author's conclusion.

CHAPTER

4

WHAT WORDS OR PHRASES ARE AMBIGUOUS?

The first three chapters of this book help you identify the basic structural elements in any message. At this point, if you can locate a writer's or speaker's conclusion and reasons, you are progressing rapidly toward the ultimate goal of forming your own rational decisions. Your next step is to put this structural picture into even clearer focus.

While identifying the conclusion and reasons gives you the basic visible structure, you still need to examine the precise *meaning* of these parts before you can react fairly to the ideas being presented. Now you need to pay special attention to the details of the language.

Identifying the precise meaning of key words or phrases is an essential step in deciding whether to agree with someone's opinion. If you fail to check for the meaning of crucial terms and phrases, you may react to an opinion the author never intended.

Let's see why knowing the meaning of a communicator's terms is so important.

> Tourism is getting out of control. Tourism can be good for the economy, but it can also harm the locale and its residents. We need to do more to regulate tourism. If we keep allowing these people to do whatever they please, surely we as residents will suffer.

Notice that it is very hard to know what to think about this argument until we know more about the kinds of regulations that the person has in mind. A quota for tourists? A set of rules about the behavior expected of tourists? Restrictions on the part of the neighborhood that tourists are allowed to visit? We just do not know what to think until we know more about these regulations the person is suggesting.

This example illustrates an important point: You cannot react to an argument unless you understand the meanings (explicit or implied) of crucial terms and phrases. How these are interpreted will often affect the acceptability of the reasoning. Consequently, before you can determine the extent to which you wish to accept one conclusion or another, you must first attempt to discover the precise meaning of the conclusion and the reasons. While their meaning typically *appears* obvious, it often is not.

The discovery and clarification of meaning require conscious, step-by-step procedures. This chapter suggests one set of such procedures. It focuses on the following question:

 Critical Question: **What words or phrases are ambiguous?**

The Confusing Flexibility of Words

Our language is highly complex. If each word had only one potential meaning about which we all agreed, effective communication would be more likely. However, most words have more than one meaning.

Consider the multiple meanings of such words as *freedom, obscenity,* and *happiness.* These multiple meanings can create serious problems in determining the worth of an argument. For example, when someone argues that a magazine should not be published because it is *obscene,* you cannot evaluate the argument until you know what the writer means by "obscene." In this brief argument, it is easy to find the conclusion and the supporting reason, but the quality of the reasoning is difficult to judge because of the ambiguous use of *obscene.* A warning: *We often misunderstand what we read or hear because we presume that the meaning of words is obvious.*

Whenever you are reading or listening, force yourself to *search for ambiguity;* otherwise, you may simply miss the point. A term or phrase is ambiguous when its meaning is so uncertain in the context of the argument we are examining that we need further clarification before we can judge the adequacy of the reasoning.

When any of us is ambiguous, we have not necessarily done something either unfair or improper. In fact, many documents, like constitutions, are intentionally left ambiguous so that the document can evolve as different meanings of key terms become practical necessities. Indeed, because we rely on words to get our points across when we communicate, there is no way to avoid ambiguity. But what can and should be avoided is ambiguity in an argument. When someone is trying to persuade us to believe or do something, that person has a responsibility to clarify any potential ambiguity before we consider the worth of the reasoning.

Locating Key Terms and Phrases

The first step in determining which terms or phrases are ambiguous is to use the stated issue as a clue for possible key terms. Key terms or phrases will be those terms that may have more than one plausible meaning within the context of the issue; that is, terms that you know must be clarified before you can decide to agree or disagree with the communicator. To illustrate the potential benefit of checking the meaning of terminology in the stated issue, let's examine several issues:

1. Does TV violence adversely affect society?
2. Is the Miss America contest demeaning to women?
3. Is the incidence of rape in college residence halls increasing?

> **Attention:**   Ambiguity refers to the existence of multiple possible meanings for a word or phrase.

Each of these stated issues contains phrases that writers or speakers will have to make clear before you will be able to evaluate their response to the issue. Each of the following phrases is potentially ambiguous: "TV violence," "adversely affect society," "demeaning to women," and "incidence of rape." Thus, when you read an essay responding to these issues, you will want to pay close attention to how the author has defined these terms.

The next step in determining which terms or phrases are ambiguous is to identify what words or phrases seem crucial in determining how well the author's reasons support her conclusion; that is, to identify the *key* terms in the reasoning structure. Once you locate these terms, you can then determine whether their meaning is ambiguous.

When searching for key terms and phrases, you should keep in mind why you are looking. Someone wants you to accept a conclusion. Therefore, you are looking for only those terms or phrases that will affect whether you accept the conclusion. *So, look for them in the reasons and conclusion.* Terms and phrases that are not included in the basic reasoning structure can thus be "dumped from your pan."

Another useful guide for searching for key terms and phrases is to keep in mind the following rule: The more abstract a word or phrase, the more likely it is to be susceptible to multiple interpretations. To avoid being unclear in our use of the term *abstract*, we define it here in the following way: A term becomes more and more abstract as it refers less and less to particular, specific instances. Thus, the words *equality, responsibility, pornography,* and *aggression* are much more abstract than are the phrases "having equal access to necessities of life," "directly causing an event," "pictures of male and female genitals," and "doing deliberate physical harm to another person." These latter phrases provide a much more concrete picture and are therefore less ambiguous.

You can also locate potential important ambiguous phrases by *reverse role-playing.* Ask yourself, if you were to *adopt a position contrary to the author's,* would you choose to define certain terms or phrases differently? If so, you have identified a possible ambiguity. For example, someone who sees beauty pageants as desirable is likely to define "demeaning to women" quite differently from someone who sees them as undesirable.

Summary of Clues for Locating Key Terms

1. Review the issue for possible key terms.

2. Look for crucial words or phrases within the reasons and conclusion.

3. Keep an eye out for abstract words and phrases.

4. Use reverse role-playing to determine how someone might define certain words and phrases differently.

Checking for Ambiguity

You now know where to look for ambiguous terms or phrases. The next step is to focus on each term or phrase and ask yourself, "Do I understand its meaning?" In answering this very important question, you will need to overcome several major obstacles.

One obstacle is assuming that you and the author mean the same thing. Thus, you need to begin your search by avoiding "mind reading." You need to get into the habit of asking, "What do you mean by that?" instead of, "I know just what you mean." A second obstacle is assuming that terms have a single, obvious definition. Many terms do not. Thus, always ask, "Could any of the words or phrases have a different meaning?"

You can be certain you have identified an especially important unclear term by performing the following test. If you can express two or more alternative meanings for a term, each of which makes sense in the context of the argument, and if the extent to which a reason would support a conclusion is affected by which meaning is assumed, then you have located a significant ambiguity. Thus, a good test for determining whether you have identified an important ambiguity is to *substitute* the alternative meanings into the reasoning structure and see whether changing the meaning *makes a difference* in how well a reason supports the conclusion.

USING THIS CRITICAL QUESTION

The preceding paragraph deserves your full attention. It is spelling out a procedure for putting this critical question about ambiguity to work. Once you have followed the procedure, you can demonstrate to yourself or anyone else why the reasoning needs more work. Try as you might to want to believe what is being said, you just cannot, as a critical thinker, agree with the reasoning until the ambiguity that affects the reasoning is repaired.

Determining Ambiguity

Let's now apply the above hints to help us determine which key terms a communicator has left unclear. *Remember:* As we do this exercise, keep asking, "What does the author mean by that?" and pay particular attention to abstract terms.

We will start with a simple reasoning structure: an advertisement.

OurBrand Sleep Aid: Works great in just 30 min.

Issue: *What sleep aid should you buy?*

Conclusion: (implied): *Buy OurBrand Sleep Aid.*

Reason: *Works great in 30 min.*

The phrases "Buy OurBrand Sleep Aid" and "in 30 min" seem quite concrete and self-evident. But, how about "works great?" Is the meaning obvious? We think not. How do we know? Let's perform a test together. Could "works great" have more than one meaning? Yes. It could mean the pill makes you drowsy. It could mean the pill completely knocks you out such that you will have difficulty waking up the next morning. Or it could have many other meanings. Isn't it true that you would be more eager to follow the advice of the advertisement if the pill worked great, meaning it works precisely as you want it to work? Thus, the ambiguity is significant because it affects the degree to which you might be persuaded by the advertisement.

Advertising is often full of ambiguity. Advertisers intentionally engage in ambiguity to persuade you that their products are superior to those of their competitors. Here are some sample advertising claims that are ambiguous. See if you can identify alternative, plausible meanings for the italicized words or phrases.

> No-Pain is the *extra-strength* pain reliever.

> Here is a book at last that shows you how to find and keep a *good man*.

In each case, the advertiser hoped that you would assign the most attractive meaning to the ambiguous words. Critical reading can sometimes protect you from making purchasing decisions that you would later regret.

Let's now look at a more complicated example of ambiguity. Remember to begin by identifying the issue, conclusion, and reasons. Resist the temptation to make note of the unclear meaning of any and all words. Only the ambiguity **in the reasoning** is crucial to critical thinkers.

We absolutely must put limits on tanning. Tanning is a substantial health risk with severe consequences. Studies have shown that those who tan are at a higher risk of skin diseases as a result of tanning.

Let's examine the reasoning for any words or phrases that would affect our willingness to accept it.

First, let's examine the issue for terms we will want the author to make clear. Certainly, we would not be able to agree or disagree with this author's conclusion until she has indicated what she means by "tanning," does she mean tanning outdoors or artificial tanning? Thus, we will want to check how clearly she has defined it in her reasoning.

Next, let's list all key terms and phrases in the conclusion and reasons: "health risk," "severe consequences," "studies have shown," "those who tan are at a higher risk," "skin diseases," and "we should put limits on tanning." Let's take a close look at a few of these to determine whether they could have different meanings that might make a difference in how we would react to the reasoning.

First, her conclusion is ambiguous. Exactly what does it mean to "put limits on tanning"? Does it mean to prevent people from using artificial tanning devices, or might it mean putting a limit on the amount of time spent tanning? Before you could decide whether to agree with the speaker or writer, you would first have to decide what it is she wants us to believe.

Next, she argues that "those who tan are at a higher risk of skin diseases." We have already talked about how we are not sure what she means by "those who tan," but what does she mean by "skin diseases?" She could mean any number of irritations that can occur from sun exposure or she could be talking about something as severe as skin cancer. It is significant to know which of these she was addressing if she wanted to convince you of the dangers of tanning and her conclusion to limit it. Try to create a mental picture of what these phrases represent. If you can't, the phrases are ambiguous. If different images would cause you to react to the reasons differently, you have identified an important ambiguity.

Now, check the other phrases we listed above. Do they not also need to be clarified? You can see that if you accept this writer's argument without requiring her to clarify these ambiguous phrases, you will not have understood what it is you agreed to believe.

Context and Ambiguity

Writers and speakers only rarely define their terms. Thus, typically your only guide to the meaning of an ambiguous statement is the context in which the words are used. By *context*, we mean the writer's or speaker's background, traditional uses of the term within the particular controversy, and the words and statements preceding and following the possible ambiguity. All three elements provide clues to the meaning of a potential key term or phrase.

If you were to see the term *human rights* in an essay, you should immediately ask yourself, "What rights are those?" If you examine the context and find that the writer is a leading member of the Norwegian government, it is a good bet that the human rights she has in mind are the rights to be employed, receive free health care, and obtain adequate housing. An American senator might mean something very different by human rights. She could have in mind freedoms of speech, religion, travel, and peaceful assembly. Notice that the two versions of human rights are not necessarily consistent. A country could guarantee one form of human rights and at the same time violate the other. You must try to clarify such terms by examining their context.

Writers frequently make clear their assumed meaning for a term by their arguments. The following paragraph is an example:

> The amusement park has given great satisfaction to most of its customers. More than half of the people surveyed agreed that the park had a wide variety of games and rides and that they would return to the park soon.

The phrase "give great satisfaction" is potentially ambiguous, because it could have a variety of meanings. However, the writer's argument makes clear that in this context, "give great satisfaction" means having a variety of games and rides.

Note that, even in this case, you would want some further clarification before you travel to this park, because "having a variety of games" is ambiguous. Wouldn't you want to know perhaps how many rides or games there were, or what some of them were? It is possible that while there is a wide variety of games, all of them are outdated or not popular anymore?

USING THIS CRITICAL QUESTION

The critical question focusing on ambiguity provides you with a fair-minded basis for disagreeing with the reasoning. If you and the person trying to persuade you are using different meanings for key terms in the reasoning, you would have to work out those disagreements first before you could accept the reasoning being offered to you.

Examine the context carefully to determine the meaning of key terms and phrases. If the meaning remains uncertain, you have located an important ambiguity. If the meaning is clear and you disagree with it, then you should be wary of any reasoning that involves that term or phrase.

Ambiguity, Definitions, and the Dictionary

It should be obvious from the preceding discussion that to locate and clarify ambiguity, you must be aware of the possible meanings of words. Meanings usually come in one of three forms: synonyms, examples, and what we will call "definition by specific criteria." For example, one could offer at least three different definitions of *anxiety*:

1. Anxiety is feeling nervous (*synonym*).
2. Anxiety is what the candidate experienced when he turned on the television to watch the election returns (*example*).
3. Anxiety is a subjective feeling of discomfort accompanied by increased sensitivity of the autonomic nervous system (*specific criteria*).

For critical evaluation of most controversial issues, synonyms and examples are inadequate. They fail to tell you the specific properties that are crucial for an unambiguous understanding of the term. Useful definitions are those that specify criteria for usage—and the more specific the better.

Where do you go for your definitions? One obvious and very important source is your dictionary. However, dictionary definitions frequently consist of synonyms, examples, or incomplete specifications of criteria for usage. These definitions often do not adequately define the use of a term in a particular essay. In such cases, you must discover possible meanings from the context of the passage, or from what else you know about the topic. We suggest you keep a dictionary handy, but keep in mind that the appropriate definition may not be there.

Let's take a closer look at some of the inadequacies of a dictionary definition. Examine the following brief paragraph.

> The quality of education at this university is not declining. In my interviews, I found that an overwhelming majority of the students and instructors responded that they saw no decline in the quality of education here.

It is clearly important to know what is meant by "quality of education" in the above paragraph. If you look up the word *quality* in the dictionary, you will find many meanings, the most appropriate, given this context, being *excellence* or *superiority*. *Excellence* and *superiority* are synonyms for quality—and they are equally abstract. You still need to know precisely what is meant by *excellence* or *superiority*. How do you know whether education is high in quality or excellence? Ideally, you would want the writer to tell you precisely what *behaviors* she is referring to when she uses the phrase "quality of education." Can you think of some different ways that the phrase might be defined? The following list presents some possible definitions of *quality of education*:

average grade-point average of students

ability of students to think critically

number of professors who have doctoral degrees

amount of work usually required to pass an exam

Each of these definitions suggests a different way to measure quality; each specifies a different criterion. Each provides a concrete way in which the term could be used. Note also that each of these definitions will affect the degree to which you will want to agree with the author's reasoning. For example, if you believe that "quality" should refer to the ability of students to think critically, and most of the students in the interviews are defining it as how much work is required to pass an exam, the reason would not *necessarily* support the conclusion. Exams may not require the ability to think critically.

Thus, in many arguments you will not be able to find adequate dictionary definitions, and the context may not make the meaning clear. One way to discover possible alternative meanings is to try to create a mental picture of what the words represent. If you cannot do so, then you probably have identified an important ambiguity. Let's apply such a test to the following example:

> Our company has had many competent employees. If you join our staff, you will start immediately at the rate we discussed with, of course, added benefits. I hope you consider all these factors in making your employment decision.

This is clearly an argument to persuade someone to work at his or her place of employment. The reasons are the salary and "added benefits." Can you create a single clear mental picture of "added benefits?" We each have some such idea, but it is highly unlikely that the ideas are identical; indeed, they may be quite different. Do "added benefits" refer to health care insurance or a new corner office? For us to evaluate the argument, we would need to know more about the meaning the writer has for "added benefits." Thus, we have located an important ambiguity.

Ambiguity and Loaded Language

Ambiguity is not always an accident. Those trying to persuade you are often quite aware that words have multiple meanings. Furthermore, they know that certain of those meanings carry with them heavy emotional baggage. Words like *sacrifice* and *justice* have multiple meanings, and some of those meanings are loaded in the sense that they stimulate certain emotions in us. Anyone trying to use language to lead us by the heart can take advantage of these probable emotions.

For example, the American military officials who control prisons in Afghanistan and Guantanomo are eager to avoid the appearance that these prisons encourage a large number of suicides among the prisoners. Yet a large number of prisoners do take their own lives. The military have to count those deaths somehow. So they have created categories like "Self-inflicted Hazardous Incidents" that permit them to acknowledge the deaths without putting them into the category of suicides. Here the ambiguity of "Self-inflicted Hazardous Incidents" is far from accidental.

Political language is often loaded and ambiguous. For example, *welfare* is often how we refer to governmental help to those we don't like; when help from the government goes to groups we like, we call it a *subsidy* or an *incentive*. The following table consists of political terms and the intended emotional impact.

Ambiguous Political Language	
Term	Emotional Impact
Revenue enhancement	Positive response to tax hikes
Tax and spend democrats	Irresponsible and wasteful
Restoring fairness	Approval of proposed tax changes
Extreme	Undesirable, unreasonable
Terrorist	Wild, crazy, uncivilized
Defense spending	Protective, required
Reform	Desirable changes

All the terms in the table are ambiguous. As critical thinkers, we must be sensitive to their intended emotional impact and the role of ambiguity in encouraging that impact. By searching for alternative meanings of terms such as *reform*, we can safeguard ourselves against easy emotional commitments to arguments we would otherwise question. After all, even the most dangerous political change is in some sense a "reform."

Norman Solomon's *The Power of Babble* provides a colorful illustration of how successful politicians use ambiguous language to persuade others. Note that Mr. Solomon has conveniently placed key ambiguous terms in alphabetical order for us.

America is back, and bipartisan—biting the bullet with competitiveness, diplomacy, efficiency, empowerment, end games, and environmentalism, along with faith in the founding Fathers, freedom's blessings, free markets and free peoples, and most of all, God. Our great heritage has held the line for human rights, individual initiative, justice, kids, leadership, liberty, loyalty, mainstream values, the marketplace, measured responses, melting pots, the middle class, military reform, moderates, modernization, moral standards, national security, and Old Glory. Opportunity comes from optimism, patriotism, peace through strength, the people, pluralism, and points of light. Pragmatism and the power of prayer make for principle while the private sector protects the public interest. Realism can mean recycling, self-discipline, and the spirit of '76, bring stability and standing tall for strategic interests and streamlined taxation. Uncle Sam has been undaunted ever since Valley Forge, with values venerated by veterans; vigilance, vigor, vision, voluntarism, and Western values. (p. 3)

Limits of Your Responsibility to Clarify Ambiguity

After you have attempted to identify and clarify ambiguity, what can you do if you are still uncertain about the meaning of certain key ideas? What is a reasonable next step? We suggest you ignore any reason containing ambiguity that makes it impossible to judge the acceptability of the reason. It is your responsibility as an active learner to ask questions that clarify ambiguity. However, your responsibility stops at that point. It is the writer or speaker who is trying to convince you of something. Her role as a persuader requires her to respond to your concerns about possible ambiguity.

You are not required to react to unclear ideas or options. If a friend tells you that you should enroll in a class because it "really is different," but cannot tell you how it is different, then you have no basis for agreeing or disagreeing with the advice. No one has the right to be believed if he cannot provide you with a clear picture of his reasoning.

Ambiguity and Your Own Writing and Speaking

Although most of this chapter is addressed to you as a critical reader and listener, it is also extremely relevant to improved writing and speaking. Effective communicators strive for clarity. They review what they intend to say several times, looking for any statements that might be ambiguous.

Look back at the section on "Locating Key Terms and Phrases" (p. 39). Use the hints given there for finding important ambiguity to revise your own efforts to communicate. For instance, abstractions that are ambiguous can be clarified by providing specific criteria for the use of the abstraction or by concrete illustrations, conveying the meaning you intend. Pay special attention to your own reasons and conclusions; try to rid them of ambiguity out of respect for your audience. When you fear ambiguity of expression, carefully define your terms.

Thinking about the characteristics of your intended audience can help you decide where ambiguities need to be clarified. A specialized audience may adequately understand jargon or specific abstractions that would be very ambiguous to a general audience. Remember that your audience will probably not struggle for a long time with your meaning. If you confuse a member of your audience, you will probably lose him quickly. If you never regain his attention, then you have failed in your task as a communicator.

Take another look at the previous section discussing the burden of responsibility surrounding the use of ambiguity. It is you the writer or speaker who must bear that burden; it is you who is attempting to convince someone else.

Summary

You cannot evaluate an essay until you know the communicator's intended meaning of key terms and phrases as well as alternative meanings they could conceivably have had in the context of the argument. You can find important clues to potential ambiguity in the statement of the issue and can locate key words and phrases in the reasons and conclusions. Because many authors fail to define their terms and because many key terms have multiple meanings, you must search for possible ambiguity. You do this by asking the questions, "What *could* be meant?" and "What *is* meant by the key terms?" Once you have completed the search, you will know four very important components of the reasoning:

1. the key terms and phrases;
2. which of these are adequately defined;
3. which of these possess other possible definitions, which if substituted, would modify your reaction to the reasoning; and
4. which of these are ambiguous within the context of the argument.

Practice Exercises

Critical Question: **What words or phrases are ambiguous?**

In the following passages, identify examples of ambiguity. Try to explain why the examples harm the reasoning.

Passage 1

School dress codes are limits put on inappropriate clothing to help keep the learning environment focused. It can be quite a distraction for students if a classmate has inappropriate clothing. The use of a dress code during school is not preventing freedom of expression. The dress code still allows for students to choose what they wear as long as it is not deemed inappropriate, unlike required uniform dress codes.

Passage 2

We should treat drug use in the same way we treat speech and religion, as a fundamental right. No one has to ingest any drug he does not want, just as no one has to read a particular book. The only reason the state assumes control over such matters is to subjugate its citizens—by shielding them from temptations as befits children.

Passage 3

Note: This passage is adapted from an opinion delivered by Chief Justice Warren Burger in a Supreme Court response concerning the constitutionality of a Georgia obscenity statute.

We categorically disapprove the theory, apparently adopted by the trial judge, that obscene, pornographic films acquire constitutional immunity from state regulation simply because they are exhibited for consenting adults only. This holding was properly rejected by the Georgia Supreme Court. . . . In particular, we hold that there are legitimate state interests at stake in stemming the tide of commercialized obscenity, even assuming it is feasible to enforce effective safeguards against exposure to juveniles and passersby. Rights and interests other than those of the advocates are involved. These include the interest of the public in the quality of life and the total community environment, the tone of commerce in the great city centers, and possibly, the public safety itself . . .

The sum of experience, including that of the past two decades, affords an ample basis for legislatures to conclude that a sensitive, key relationship of human existence, central to family life, community welfare and the development of human personality, can be debased and distorted by crass commercial exploitation of sex.

Sample Responses

Passage 1

ISSUE: *Should schools have dress codes?*

CONCLUSION: *Yes, schools should have dress codes.*

REASONS: 1. *Certain dress codes keep the learning environment focused.*
             2. *The school is not preventing freedom of expression by implementing a dress code.*

What are the key phrases in this reasoning? They are: "dress codes," "inappropriate clothing," and "freedom of expression." You would first want to determine the meaning of each of these phrases. Is it clear what is meant by inappropriate clothing? No. The limited context provided fails to reveal an adequate definition. If inappropriate clothing refers to the cut of skirts or to clothing with obscenities printed on them, wouldn't you be more likely to accept the reasoning than if the author included wearing sandals? Can you tell from the argument whether the author is referring to whatever the administration deems inappropriate or only to a few standard dress code issues commonly seen in schools? To be able to agree or to disagree with the author requires in this instance a more careful definition of what is meant by "inappropriate clothing." Notice that "dress codes" and "freedom of expression" need further clarification before you can decide whether to agree with the author.

Passage 2

ISSUE: *Should the state regulate drug use?*

CONCLUSION: *Drug use should not be regulated by the state.*

REASONS: 1. *Just as freedom of speech and religion, drug use is a fundamental right.*
             2. *State control subjugates citizens by not permitting them to take responsibility for voluntary acts.*

What are the key phrases in this reasoning? They are: "drug use," "fundamental right," and "subjugate citizens." You would first want to determine the meaning of each of these phrases. Is it clear what is meant by drug use? No. The limited context provided fails to reveal an adequate definition. If drug use refers to the ingestion of drugs that are not considered highly addictive, such as marijuana, wouldn't you be more likely to accept the reasoning than if the author included heroin within her definition of drugs? Can you tell from the argument whether the author is referring to all drugs or only to a subset of currently regulated drugs? To be able to agree or to disagree with the author requires in this instance a more careful definition of what is meant by "drug use." Notice that "fundamental right" and "subjugate citizens" need further clarification before you can decide whether to agree with the author.

?   CRITICAL QUESTION SUMMARY:
WHY THIS QUESTION IS IMPORTANT

What Words or Phrases Are Ambiguous?

Once you have identified an author's argument, you need to identify key words or phrases within that reasoning that might have alternative meanings. More importantly, you need to determine whether the author explicitly uses one of those definitions. If she does not, and if one of those meanings alters your acceptance of the conclusion, you have identified an important ambiguity. Identifying ambiguous words and phrases is the next important step in determining whether you will accept or reject the conclusion.

5

WHAT ARE THE VALUE CONFLICTS AND ASSUMPTIONS?

Anyone trying to convince you to believe a particular position will make an attempt to present reasons consistent with that position. Hence, at first glance almost every argument appears to "make sense." The visible structure looks good. But the visible, stated reasons are not the only ideas that serve to prove or support the conclusion. Hidden or unstated beliefs may be at least as significant in understanding the argument. Let's examine the importance of these unstated ideas by considering the following brief argument.

> Local law enforcement needs to do more to impose consequences for littering. Obviously, people are not taking enough initiative on their own to follow the laws; therefore, city police have to do something. How can we expect change without enforcement?

The reason—at first glance—supports the conclusion. If the city expects change in the behavior of its citizens, it follows that the city's law enforcement should have to enforce that change. But it is also possible that the reason given can be true and yet not *necessarily* support the conclusion. What if you believe that it is the individual's responsibility—not the collective responsibility of government—to take responsibility for the extent of littering? If so, from your perspective, the reason no longer supports the conclusion. This reasoning is convincing to you only if you agree with certain unstated ideas that the writer has taken for granted. In this case, one idea taken for granted is that collective responsibility is more desirable than individual responsibility.

In all arguments, there will be certain ideas taken for granted by the writer. Typically, these ideas will not be stated. You will have to find them by reading between the lines. These ideas are important invisible links in the reasoning structure, the glue that holds the entire argument together. Until you supply these links, you cannot truly understand the argument.

If you miss the hidden links, you will often find yourself believing something that had you been more reflective, you would never have accepted. *Remember:* the visible surface of an argument will almost always be dressed in its best clothes because the person presenting the argument wishes to encourage you to make the argument your own. This chapter can be particularly useful to you as a critical thinker because it prepares you to look at the full argument, not just its more attractive features.

As another illustration, consider why you should work hard to master the skills and attitudes contained in this book. There are all kinds of reasons why you should not learn critical thinking. Careful thought is much more demanding of our energies than would be another decision-making approach like flipping a coin or asking the nearest self-confident expert what you should think and do. But this text is encouraging you to learn critical thinking. We are telling you that critical thinking is advantageous for you.

But our advice is based on some invisible beliefs, and if you do not share those beliefs, our advice should not be followed. Critical thinkers believe that autonomy, curiosity, and reasonableness are among the most important of human objectives. (Later in this chapter, we learn to refer to ideas like autonomy, curiosity, and reasonableness as values.) The end-product of critical thinking is someone who is open to multiple points of view, assesses those perspectives with reason, and then uses that assessment to make decisions about what to believe and what actions to take. We trust that you like that portrayal of life and, consequently, that you will want to be a critical thinker.

Your task is similar in many ways to having to reproduce a magic trick without having seen how the magician did the trick. You see the handkerchief go into the hat and the rabbit come out, but you are not aware of the magician's hidden maneuvers. To understand the trick, you must discover these maneuvers. Likewise, in arguments, you must discover the hidden maneuvers, which, in actuality, are unstated ideas. We shall refer to these unstated ideas as assumptions. To fully understand an argument, you must identify the assumptions.

Assumptions are:

1. hidden or unstated (in most cases);
2. taken for granted;

3. influential in determining the conclusion; and

4. potentially deceptive.

This chapter and the next one will show you how to discover assumptions. We will focus on one kind of assumption in this chapter—value assumptions.

But identifying assumptions is more valuable than just the positive impact it has on your own reasoning. Critical thinking necessarily involves other people who are concerned about the same issues as you. When you identify assumptions and make them explicit in your interactions with others, you make a tremendous contribution to the quality of the reasoning in our community as well.

For instance, the Associated Press recently ran an account of a study from the St. Louis Federal Reserve Bank. The study concluded that good-looking people tend to make more money and get promoted more often than those who are just average looking. As a critical thinker, you can question the assumptions behind such a report and, in so doing, prevent us from quickly embracing arguments that use such data to support their conclusions. Democracy badly needs just this kind of cautious reflection.

 Critical Question: **What are the value conflicts and assumptions?**

General Guide for Identifying Assumptions

When you seek assumptions, where and how should you look? Numerous assumptions exist in any book, discussion, or article, but you need to be concerned about relatively few. As you remember, the visible structure of an argument consists of reasons and conclusions. Thus, you are interested only in assumptions that affect the quality of this structure. You can restrict your search for assumptions, therefore, to the structure you have already learned how to identify.

In particular, there are two places to look for assumptions. Look for assumptions needed for the reason(s) to support the conclusions (linkage assumptions) and look for ones necessary for a reason to be true. We first introduce you to assumptions that are extremely influential in prescriptive arguments—value assumptions. **Look for value assumptions in the movement from reasons to conclusion!**

Note that the reasons and conclusion are also the place where we search for significant ambiguity. Once again, we are showing great respect for the importance in a speech or an essay of the reasons and the conclusion.

> **Attention:** An assumption is an unstated belief that supports the explicit reasoning.

Value Conflicts and Assumptions

Why is it that some very reasonable people shout that abortion is murder, while other equally reasonable observers see abortion as humane? Have you ever wondered why every U.S. president, regardless of his political beliefs, eventually gets involved in a dispute with the press over publication of government information that he would prefer not to share? How can some highly intelligent observers attack the publication of sexually explicit magazines and others defend their publication as the ultimate test of our Bill of Rights?

One extremely important reason for these different conclusions is the existence of *value conflicts*, or the differing values that stem from different frames of reference. For ethical or prescriptive arguments, an individual's values influence the reasons he provides and, consequently, his conclusion. In fact, the reasons will logically support the conclusion only if the *value assumption* is added to the reasoning. The small argument below illustrates the role of a value assumption in a prescriptive argument.

> We should not legalize recreational drugs. Illegal drugs cause too much street violence and other crimes.

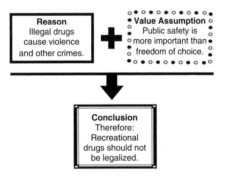

Value assumptions are very important assumptions for such arguments because they are directing the reasoning from behind a screen. The person trying to communicate with you may or may not be aware of these assumptions. You should make it a habit to identify the value assumptions on which the reasons are based.

By *value assumption*, we mean a taken-for-granted belief about the *relative desirability* of certain competing values. When authors take a position on a social controversy, they typically prefer one value over another value—they have value *priorities or preferences*. The rest of this chapter is devoted to increasing your awareness of the role played by value conflicts and value priorities in determining a person's opinions or conclusions. This awareness will help you locate and evaluate this important type of assumption.

Discovering Values

Before you can discover the importance of values in shaping conclusions, you must have some understanding of what a value is. *Values*, as we will use the term, are ideas that someone thinks are worthwhile. You will find that it is the importance one assigns to *abstract ideas* that has the major influence on one's choices and behavior.

Usually objects, experiences, and actions are desired because of some idea we value. For example, we may choose to do things that provide us with contacts with important people. We value "important people" (concrete idea) because we value "status" (abstract idea). When we use the word *value* in this chapter, we will be referring to an (abstract) idea representing what someone thinks is important and good.

> **Attention:**   Values are the unstated ideas that people see as worthwhile. They provide standards of conduct by which we measure the quality of human behavior.

To better familiarize yourself with values, write down some of your own values. Try to avoid writing down the names of people, tangible objects, or actions. Pizza and playing tennis may be important to you, but it is the importance you assign to abstract ideas that most influences your choices and behavior concerning controversial public issues. Your willingness to argue for or against capital punishment, for instance, is strongly related to the importance you assign to the sanctity of human life—an abstract idea. The sanctity of human life is a value that affects our opinions about war, abortion, drug usage, and mercy killing. As you create your list of values, focus on those that are so significant that they affect your opinions and behavior in many ways.

Did you have problems making your list? We can suggest two further aids that may help. First, another definition! Values are *standards of conduct* that we endorse and expect people to meet. When we expect our political representatives to "tell the truth," we are indicating to them and to ourselves that honesty is one of our most cherished values. Ask yourself what you expect your friends to be like. What standards of conduct would you want your children to develop? Answers to these questions should help you enlarge your understanding of values.

Now let us give you an aid for identifying values—a list of some commonly held values. Every value on our list may be an attractive candidate for your list. Thus, after you look at our list, pause for a moment and choose those values that are most important to you. They will be those values that most often play a role in shaping your opinions and behavior.

Common Values		
adventure	excellence	rationality
ambition	flexibility	security
autonomy	freedom of speech	spontaneity
collective responsibility	generosity	tolerance
comfort	harmony	tradition
competition	honesty	wisdom
cooperation	justice	
courage	novelty	
creativity	order	
equality of opportunity	peace	

From Values to Value Assumptions

To identify value assumptions, we must go beyond a simple listing of values. Others share many of your values. Wouldn't almost anyone claim that flexibility, cooperation, and honesty are desirable?

Look again at the definition, and you will immediately see that, *by definition*, most values will be on everyone's list. Because many values are shared, values by themselves are not a powerful guide to understanding. What leads you to answer a prescriptive question differently from someone else is the relative intensity with which you hold specific values.

That we attach different levels of intensity to specific values can be appreciated by thinking about responses to controversies when pairs of values collide or conflict. While it is not very enlightening to discover that most people value both competition and cooperation, we do gain a more complete understanding of prescriptive choices as we discover who *prefers* competition to cooperation when the two values conflict.

A writer's preference for particular values is often unstated, but that value preference, nevertheless, will have a major impact on her conclusion and on how she chooses to defend it. These unstated assertions about value priorities function as *value assumptions*. Some refer to these assumptions as *value judgments*. Recognition of relative support for conflicting values or sets of values provides you with both an improved understanding of what you are reading and a basis for eventual evaluation of prescriptive arguments.

When a writer takes a stand on controversial prescriptive issues, she is usually depreciating one commonly shared value while upholding another. For example, when someone advocates the required licensing of prospective parents, collective responsibility is being treated as more important than individual responsibility. So when you look for value assumptions, look for an indication of value *priorities*. Ask yourself what values are being upheld by this position and what values are being relatively downgraded in importance.

> **Attention:** A value assumption is an implicit preference for one value over another in a particular context. We use value preferences and value priorities as synonyms.

When you have found a person's value preference in a particular argument, you should not expect that same person to necessarily have the same value priority when discussing a different controversy. A person does not have the same value priorities without regard to the issue being discussed. The context and factual issues associated with a controversy also greatly influence how far we're willing to go with a particular value preference. We hold our value preferences *only up to a point*. Thus, for example, those who prefer freedom of choice over the welfare of the community in most situations (such as wearing clothing that displays an image of the flag) may shift that value preference when they see the possibility of too much damage to the welfare of the community (such as in the case of the right of a person to give a racist speech).

In other words, value assumptions are very contextual; they apply in one setting, but we may make quite a different value priority when the specifics of the prescriptive issue change. Critical thinking plays a major role in thinking deeply about whether we want to assign priority to particular values in a given instance. Because our minds tend to like to put things in neat compartments, you have to work hard to tolerate the complexity of a person's value preferences. While we can say that particular people *tend* to make particular value assumptions, we never can be certain about that presumption. Instead, we have to listen and observe closely before we can get a solid understanding of the value preferences that a person is using in a particular instance.

Typical Value Conflicts

If you are aware of typical conflicts, you can more quickly recognize the assumptions being made by a writer when she reaches a particular conclusion. We have listed some of the more common value conflicts that occur in ethical issues and have provided you with examples of controversies in which these value conflicts are likely to be evident. We anticipate that you can use this list as a starting point when you are trying to identify important value assumptions.

As you identify value conflicts, you will often find that there are several value conflicts that seem important in shaping conclusions with respect to particular controversies. When evaluating a controversy, try to find several value conflicts, as a check on yourself. Some controversies will have one primary value conflict; others may have several.

Typical Value Conflict and Sample Controversies	
1. loyalty–honesty	Should you tell your parents about your sister's drug habit?
2. competition–cooperation	Do you support the grading system?
3. freedom of press–national security	Is it wise to hold weekly presidential press conferences?
4. equality–individualism	Are racial quotas for employment fair?
5. order–freedom of speech	Should we imprison those with radical ideas?
6. security–excitement	Should you choose a dangerous profession?
7. generosity–material success	Is it desirable to give financial help to a beggar?
8. rationality–spontaneity	Should you check the odds before placing a bet?
9. tradition–novelty	Should divorces be easily available?

Take another look at number 7 in the preceding list. It is quite possible that other value conflicts besides that between generosity and material success affect your decision about whether to give financial help to a beggar. For instance, all the following value conflicts may affect a person's willingness to help a beggar:

1. individual responsibility–collective responsibility
2. competition–cooperation
3. efficiency–social stability

By identifying as many of the relevant value assumptions as possible, you have a better chance of not missing any of the important dimensions of the argument. However, you may have no way of knowing which value assumptions most influence the author's reasoning.

The Communicator's Background as a Clue to Value Assumptions

We suggested earlier that a good starting point in finding value assumptions is to check the background of the author. Find out as much as you can about the value preferences usually held by a person like the writer. Is she a corporate executive, a union leader, a Republican Party official, a doctor, or an apartment tenant? What interests does such a person naturally wish to protect? There is certainly nothing inherently wrong with pursuing self-interest, but such pursuits often limit the value assumptions a particular writer will tolerate. For example, it is highly unlikely that the president of a major automobile firm would place a high value on efficiency when a preference for efficiency rather than stability would lead to his losing his job. Consequently, you as a critical reader or listener can often quickly discover value preferences by thinking about the probable assumptions made by a person like the writer.

One caution is important. It isn't necessarily true that, because a person is a member of a group, she shares the particular value assumptions of the group. It would be a mistake to presume that every individual who belongs to a given group thinks identically. We all know that business people, farmers, and firefighters sometimes disagree among themselves when discussing particular controversies. Investigating the writer's background as a clue to her value assumptions is only a clue, and, like other clues, it can be misleading unless it is used with care.

Consequences as Clues to Value Assumptions

In prescriptive arguments, each position with respect to an issue leads to different consequences or outcomes. Each of the potential consequences will have a certain likelihood of occurring, and each will also have some level of desirability or undesirability.

How desirable a consequence is will depend on a writer's or reader's personal value preferences. The desirability of the conclusions in such cases will be dictated by the probability of the potential consequences and the importance attached to them. Thus, an important means of determining an individual's value assumptions is to examine the reasons given in support of a conclusion and then to determine what value priorities would lead to these reasons being judged as more desirable than reasons that might have been offered on the other side of the issue. Let's take a look at a concrete example.

Nuclear power plants should not be built because they will pollute our environment.

The reason provided here is a rather specific potential consequence of building nuclear plants. This writer clearly sees environmental pollution as very undesirable. Why does this consequence carry so much weight in this person's thinking? What more general value does preventing pollution help achieve? We are only guessing, but probably health or conservation are being weighted especially heavily by this person. Someone else might stress a different consequence in this argument, such as the effect on the supply of electricity to consumers. Why? Probably because he values efficiency very highly! Thus, this reason supports the conclusion *if* a value assumption is made that conservation is more important than efficiency.

Note that the *magnitude* of a consequence may have a major impact on value preferences. One may value conservation over efficiency only when efficiency may cause "significant" damage to the environment. And, one may value economic freedom over economic security only as long as unemployment stays below a given level. It is possible for people to have different conclusions, while having identical value assumptions, because they disagree about the likelihood or magnitude of consequences.

One important means of determining value assumptions, then, is to ask the question, "Why do the particular consequences or outcomes presented as reasons seem so desirable to the writer or speaker?"

Remember: When you identify *value assumptions*, you should always try to state *value priorities*. With controversial topics, stating value assumptions in this way will be a continual reminder both of what the writer is *giving up* and of what she is gaining. Try to resist the temptation to stop your analysis prematurely by just identifying the values of the speaker or writer. Identifying those values is a step on the way to finding the value assumptions, but by itself it provides very little assistance in understanding an argument. Values, by their nature, are possessed by us all.

More Hints for Finding Value Assumptions

Another useful technique for generating value conflicts is to *reverse role-play*. Ask the question, "What do those people who would take a different position from the writer's care about?" When someone argues that we should not use monkeys in experimental research, you should ask yourself, "If I wanted to defend the use of monkeys, what would I be concerned about?" Remember, when someone takes a position on a controversial topic, she will be revealing a *value priority*—a *preference for one value over another*. Your knowledge of that preference will help you to decide whether to agree with her conclusion.

Finally, you can always check to see whether the disagreement results from a value conflict concerning the *rights of an individual* to behave in a particular fashion and the *welfare of the group* affected by the behavior in question. Many arguments rest implicitly on a stance with respect to this enduring value conflict. Like other common value conflicts, we can all recall numerous instances when our thinking required us to weigh these two important values and their effects.

For example, when we wonder about the use of metal detectors in the public schools, we often begin to construct our arguments in terms of thinking about the privacy rights of the individual students *and* the threats to the student body if a student were to bring a weapon to school. Then, we try to balance those values against other values: Does the individual's right to privacy deserve greater protection than the welfare of the other students in the school in this instance? What other issues involve this value conflict? What about the request of "skinheads" to parade through ethnic neighborhoods?

Clues for Identifying Value Assumptions

1. Investigate the author's background.

2. Ask "Why do the consequences of the author's position seem so important to her?"

3. Search for similar social controversies to find analogous value assumptions.

4. Use reverse role-playing. Take a position opposite the author's position and identify which values are important to that opposite position.

5. Look for common value conflicts, such as individual responsibility versus community responsibility.

Avoiding a Typical Difficulty When Identifying Value Assumptions

Try to keep your eye on the goal of identifying value assumptions; if you stop your analysis after you have identified the primary values of the person who created the argument, you will have cut yourself off from the downside associated with the argument. Let us explain with an illustration:

> Drug research is a long, complicated, and expensive process. There are innumerable factors that researchers and medical professionals have to consider when looking for new discoveries in drugs. It is unfair for outsiders to criticize something they do not understand.
>
> Yes, prescription prices are high. But that high price actually has little to do with the cost of research. The price of prescription drugs is the responsibility of someone other than the researchers, mainly drug companies (companies that solely exist to market and sell prescription drugs). Do not punish the research companies when they ask for donations just because your prescription costs are high—the two are not related.

Suppose you read the argument and then say: I believe the person values prescription drug research. At one level, you have identified what the person who made the argument sees as important. She does indicate a desire to encourage society to fund this research. But that response is too concrete to serve as an avenue toward deeper thinking about this prescriptive issue.

To move in a more productive way toward a better understanding of the issue, take another look at the definition of values. That definition suggests a need to place drug research into a more abstract framework. Once that need is recognized, a common response is to say: She values health. That recognition is a step in the right direction. This value is at work in this argument, propelling the reasoning. The same value is relevant to any number of issues surrounding health care and the medical profession. But were we to stop at this point, we would miss much of the understanding that would emerge were we to pursue the value assumptions in the argument.

In that values are in tension with one another, we are missing a lot when we just call out the values a person has. The relative ranking of the values that affect this argument is what assists in determining the person's conclusions. That someone values the health of others over the values associated with alternative uses of public funds is what pushes them in the direction of the conclusion.

So push yourself all the way to finding value assumptions. Don't stop your search at levels of analysis that are less revealing.

Finding Value Assumptions on Your Own

Let's work on an example together to help you become more comfortable with finding value assumptions.

> Different workplaces have different working environments. Some offer competitive wages, where performance is evaluated and compared with that of others and they may or may not get a pay raise accordingly. Some places like to encourage an environment where everyone works together as a group. Pay raises in this environment are usually done by amount of education or experience. This type of workplace allows for workers to form good relationships and work together as a team. Which work environment would really have the best productivity? One where everyone was pitted against everyone else and productivity was the only basis for pay raises, or one where the environment fosters a team that works together to up the productivity?

The structure of the two positions is outlined here for you:

CONCLUSION: *The workplace should offer competitive wages.*

REASON: *The only basis for salary increases is productivity—therefore, this type of workplace creates optimal incentives for hard work.*

CONCLUSION: *The workplace should offer a team environment.*

REASON: *If the staff respects each other, they create an environment that can be healthy and effectively productive.*

Notice that the work environment where wages are based on individual productivity values competition. Those who organize that kind of environment believe that competition would create more productivity because it motivates the individual. Thus, they contend that a team environment would get in the way of the productivity of the competitive environment.

VALUE ASSUMPTION: *In this context, competition is valued over cooperation.*

On the other hand, those who think the team environment would be the most productive value cooperation. They believe that working together helps the group become motivated to be more productive, not just for themselves, but for the company (the team). They think that the group work would create a better working environment than one that offered competitive wages.

VALUE ASSUMPTION: *In this situation, cooperation is valued over competition.*

Therefore, the major value conflict is cooperation versus competition. A supporter of the competitive wage environment believes the value assumption that competition, rather than cooperation, among co-workers over pay will create the most productive environment. Her stance on this issue does not mean that she does not value cooperation; both values are probably very important to her. In the instance of the work place, however, competition has taken over.

Remember that complete reasoning with respect to prescriptive issues requires reasons *and* value assumptions.

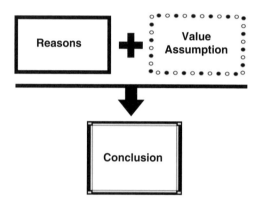

Let's complete one more example together.

Public libraries should not ban certain books. Some books are not considered to be politically correct or are considered offensive and therefore not supported by the public library system here. But their policy is hampering people's access to certain types of literature from a significant public source.

Let's first outline the structure of the argument.

CONCLUSION: *Libraries should not ban certain books.*

REASON: *People should have easy access to books of their choice at public libraries.*

What value assumption do you think would result in someone's opposition to book bans? Look back at the table on page 60. Would any of the sample value conflicts affect one's reaction to the consoling of certain books and the use of the above reasoning? Try to explain how a preference for freedom of speech over order might affect your reaction to this controversy.

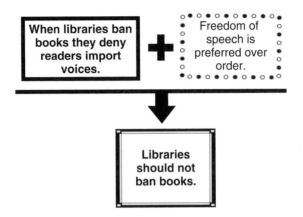

USING THIS CRITICAL QUESTION

Once you have found a value assumption, what do you do with it? First, recall the purpose of every critical question—to move you toward the evaluation of reasoning! Because you know that thoughtful people have different value assumptions, you have the right to wonder why any single value assumption is being made. Thus, as a critical thinker, you would want to point out the need for anyone who is making an argument to offer some explanation for why you should accept the particular value assumption that is implicit in that argument.

Values and Relativism

We do not want to give the impression in this chapter that value preferences are like ice cream, such that when I choose blueberry cheesecake as my flavor, you have no basis for trying to persuade me that the lemon chiffon is a better choice. Ice cream is just a matter of personal preference—end of story!

However, the choice of value preferences requires reasoning. That reasoning, like any other, can be informed, thoughtful, and caring. But it can also be sloppy and self-absorbed. Hence, value preferences require some justification that critical thinkers can consider. A value preference requires supporting reasons just as does any other conclusion. Then each of us can study the reasoning to form our own reaction.

Summary

Assumptions are unstated ideas, taken for granted in the reasoning. Within the context of social controversies, they consist of a preference for one value over another in a particular context. The author's background, reaction to projected consequences of acting on a particular value assumption, analogous controversies, and reverse role-playing all provide possible clues for finding a person's value assumptions in a particular controversy.

Practice Exercises

(?) *Critical Question:* **What are the value conflicts and assumptions?**

Identify the value conflicts that could lead to agreement or disagreement with the following points of view; then identify the value priorities assumed by the writer.

Passage 1

Sometimes it is not always best to be completely honest. Some conclusions are better left unsaid. For instance, if you are talking to a friend and he asks for your opinion about something, the truth should be avoided if there is no way to deliver it without harming the relationship.

The truth is not always necessary. If you were a doctor and you had to give your patient bad health news, then it is important to maintain honesty. However sometimes, in the case of friendship, the honesty may need some buffering.

Passage 2

Graffiti should be considered art. It seems that a lot of people associate graffiti with gang related activities, but that linkage is not always true. Graffiti is an expression of art, just as any other work by recognized artists: the canvas is just different. When graffiti damages property there is a problem, but if there were designated places for this art, then the people who are creating it would be less likely to deface the property of others.

Passage 3

Eating healthy is important. Doctors and physical fitness advisors tell you about all the advantages of health foods. Then why are these foods so expensive? Companies selling these foods are raising prices for simple things such as fruits and vegetables. Six dollars for a bag of salad should be an indicator that the prices are too high. People want to be healthy, but it seems as if corporate America really does not want to make that prospect cheap. You should avoid wasting money just to eat healthy; go buy those cheap frozen vegetables at the grocery store!

Sample Responses

Passage 1

CONCLUSION: *Lying to spare someone's feelings is appropriate in certain situations.*

REASON: *Telling the truth could harm a friendship.*

One value conflict that relates to this argument is that between honesty and harmony. Of course, others would argue that honesty is the best foundation for the kind of friendship they seek. A value preference for harmony over honesty links the reason to the conclusion.

As with most prescriptive controversies, more than one value conflict is involved in this dilemma. For example, this controversy also requires us to think about comfort over courage.

Passage 2

CONCLUSION: *Graffiti should be treated as an art form.*

REASONS: 1. *Graffiti is not always gang related; there are other motivators.*
            2. *Graffiti is an artist's expression, just not on a traditional canvas.*

A value assumption is that of freedom of expression over order. The author believes that graffiti does not unduly harm the public. If one valued order over freedom of expression, one might well reject the reasoning suggested in this passage.

 CRITICAL QUESTION SUMMARY: WHY THIS QUESTION IS IMPORTANT

What Are the Value Conflicts and Assumptions?

While an author usually offers explicit reasons why she comes to a certain conclusion, she also makes certain assumptions that lead her to a certain conclusion. By identifying value conflicts, you determine whether the author's value preferences match your value preferences. Consequently, you have a tool for determining whether you will accept or reject an author's conclusion.

WHAT ARE THE DESCRIPTIVE ASSUMPTIONS?

You should now be able to identify value assumptions—very important hidden components of prescriptive arguments. When you find value assumptions, you know pretty well what a writer or speaker wants the world to be like—what goals she thinks are most important. But you do not know what she takes for granted about the nature of the world and the people who inhabit it. Are they basically lazy or achievement oriented, cooperative or competitive, and rational or whimsical? Her visible reasoning depends on these ideas, as well as upon her values. Such unstated ideas are descriptive assumptions, and they too are essential hidden elements of an argument.

The following brief argument about a car depends on hidden assumptions. Can you find them?

> This car will get you to your destination, whatever it may be. I have driven this model of car on multiple occasions.

This chapter focuses on the identification of descriptive assumptions.

(?) *Critical Question:* **What are the descriptive assumptions?**

Descriptive assumptions are beliefs about the way the world is; prescriptive or value assumptions, you remember, are beliefs about how the world should be.

Illustrating Descriptive Assumptions

Let's examine our argument about the car to illustrate more clearly what we mean by a descriptive assumption.

The reasoning structure is:

CONCLUSION: *This particular car will get you where you want to go.*

REASON: *This model of car has functioned well on multiple occasions.*

The reasoning thus far is incomplete. We know that, *by itself,* a reason just does not have the strength to support a conclusion; the reason must be connected to the conclusion by certain other (frequently unstated) ideas. These ideas, if true, justify treating the reason as support for the conclusion. Thus, whether a reason supports, or is relevant to, a conclusion depends on whether we can locate unstated ideas that logically connect the reason to the conclusion. When such unstated ideas are descriptive, we call them *descriptive assumptions.* Let us present two such assumptions for the above argument.

ASSUMPTION 1: *From year to year a particular model of car has a consistent quality.*

First, no such statement was provided in the argument itself. However, if the reason is true and if this assumption is true, then the reason provides some support for the conclusion. But if not all model years have the same level of dependability (and we know they do not), then experience with a model in previous years cannot be a reliable guide to whether one should buy the car in the current model year. Note that this assumption is a statement about the way things are, not about the way things *should be.* Thus, it is a *descriptive connecting assumption.*

ASSUMPTION 2: *The driving that would be done with the new car is the same kind of driving that was done by the person recommending the car.*

When we speak about "driving" a car, the ambiguity of driving can get us into trouble if we do not clarify the term. If the "driving" of the person recommending the car refers to regular trips to the grocery store on a quiet suburban street with no hills, that driving experience is not very relevant as a comparator when the new car is to be driven in Colorado, while pulling a heavy trailer. Thus, this conclusion is supported by the reason only if a certain definition of driving is assumed.

We can call this kind of descriptive assumption a *definitional assumption* because we have taken for granted one meaning of a term that could have more than one meaning. Thus, one important kind of descriptive assumption to look for is a *definitional assumption*—the taking for granted of one meaning

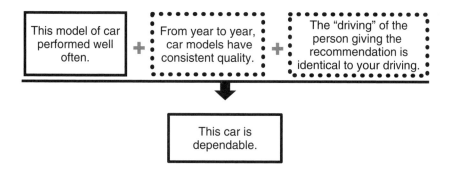

for a term that has multiple possible meanings. Let's see what this process looks like in argument form:

Once you have identified the connecting assumptions, you have answered the question, "On what basis can that conclusion be drawn from that reason?" The next natural step is to ask, "Is there any basis for accepting the assumptions?" If not, then, for you, the reason fails to provide support for the conclusion. If so, then the reason provides logical support for the conclusion. Thus, you can say reasoning is sound when you have identified connecting assumptions and you have good reason to believe those assumptions.

Attention: A descriptive assumption is an unstated belief about how the world was, is, or will become.

When you identify assumptions, you identify ideas the communicator *needs* to take for granted so that the reason is supportive of the conclusion. Because writers and speakers frequently are not aware of their own assumptions, their conscious beliefs may be quite different from the ideas you identify as implicit assumptions. When you then make the hidden connecting tissue of an argument visible, you also contribute to their understanding of their own argument and may thereby guide them to better beliefs and decisions.

USING THIS CRITICAL QUESTION

After you have found descriptive assumptions, you want to think about whether there is a strong basis for accepting them. It is certainly fair for you to expect the person making the argument to provide you with some justification for why you should accept these particular assumptions. Finally, if the assumption is not supported and you find it questionable, you are behaving responsibly when you decide not to buy the argument. Your point in rejecting it is not to disagree with the conclusion. Instead, you are saying that you cannot accept the conclusion *based on the reasons offered so far*. In other words, you are quite willing to believe what you are being told, but as a critical thinker you are in the business of personal development. That development can take place only when you accept only those conclusions that have persuasive reasons.

Clues for Locating Assumptions

Your task in finding assumptions is to reconstruct the reasoning by filling in the missing links. You want to provide ideas that help the communicator's reasoning "make sense." Once you have a picture of the entire argument, both the visible and the invisible parts, you will be in a much better position to determine its strengths and weaknesses.

How does one go about finding these important missing links? It requires hard work, imagination, and creativity. Finding important assumptions is a difficult task.

You have been introduced to two types of assumptions—value assumptions and descriptive assumptions. In the previous chapter, we gave you several hints for finding value assumptions. Here are some clues that will make your search for descriptive assumptions successful.

Keep thinking about the gap between the conclusion and reasons.   Why are you looking for assumptions in the first place? You are looking because you want to be able to judge how well the reasons support the conclusions. Thus, look for what the writer or speaker would have had to take for granted to link the reasons and conclusion. Keep asking, *"How do you get from the reason to the conclusion?"* Ask, *"If the reason is true, what else must be true for the conclusion to follow?"* And, to help answer that question, you will find it very helpful to ask, *"Supposing the reason(s) were true, is there any way in which the conclusion nevertheless could be false?"*

Searching for the gap will be helpful for finding both value and descriptive assumptions.

Look for ideas that support reasons.   Sometimes a reason is presented with no explicit support; yet the plausibility of the reason depends on the acceptability of ideas that have been taken for granted. These ideas are descriptive assumptions. The following brief argument illustrates such a case:

CONCLUSION: *All high-school English classes will go see at least one Shakespeare play.*

REASON: *It is beneficial to experience Shakespeare's works first hand.*

What ideas must be taken for granted for this reason to be acceptable? We must assume:

(a) The performance will be well done and reflective of what Shakespeare would encourage, and

(b) students will understand the play and be able to relate it to Shakespeare.

Both (a) and (b) are ideas that have to be taken for granted for the reasons to be acceptable and, thus, supportive of the conclusion.

Identify with the writer or speaker.   Locating someone's assumptions is often made easier by imagining that you were asked to defend the conclusion. If you can, crawl into the skin of a person who would reach such a conclusion. Discover his background. Whether the person whose conclusion you are evaluating is a corporate executive, a labor leader, a boxing promoter, or a judge, try to play the role of such a person and plan in your mind what he would be thinking as he moves toward the conclusion. When an executive for a coal company argues that strip mining does not significantly harm the beauty of our natural environment, he has probably begun with a belief that strip mining is beneficial to our nation. Thus, he may assume a definition of beauty that would be consistent with his arguments, while other definitions of beauty would lead to a condemnation of strip mining.

Identify with the opposition.   If you are unable to locate assumptions by taking the role of the speaker or writer, try to reverse roles. Ask yourself why anyone might disagree with the conclusion. What type of reasoning would prompt someone to disagree with the conclusion you are evaluating? If you can play the role of a person who would not accept the conclusion, you can more readily see assumptions in the explicit structure of the argument.

Recognize the potential existence of other means of attaining the advantages referred to in the reasons.   Frequently, a conclusion is supported by reasons that indicate the various advantages of acting on the author's conclusion. When there are many ways to reach the same advantages, one important assumption linking the reasons to the conclusion is that the best way to attain the advantages is through the one advocated by the communicator.

Let's try this technique with one brief example. Experts disagree about how a person should establish financial stability. Many times young people are encouraged to establish credit with a credit card. But aren't there many ways to establish financial stability? Might not some of these alternatives have less serious disadvantages than those that could result when a young person spends too much on that credit card? For example, investing some money in a savings account or establishing credit by maintaining a checking account are viable routes to establishing financial stability. Thus, those who suggest that people get credit cards to help establish financial stability are not taking into account the risks involved with their solution or the possibility of fewer risks with an alternative.

Avoid stating incompletely established reasons as assumptions. When you first attempt to locate assumptions you may find yourself locating a stated reason, thinking that the reason has not been adequately established, and asserting, "That's only an assumption. You don't know that to be the case." Or you might simply restate the reason as the assumption. You may have correctly identified a need on the part of the writer or speaker to better establish the truth of her reason. While this clarification is an important insight on your part, you have not identified an assumption in the sense that we have been using it in these two chapters. You are simply labeling a reason "an assumption."

Here is an example of stating an incompletely established reason as an assumption.

> The ratings are going through the roof for Science Fiction shows. The advertising agencies have done a great job.

Now, challenge the argument by identifying the following assumption: The writer is assuming that advertising is causing the ratings to rise.

Do you see that when you do this, all you are doing is stating that the author's reason is her assumption—when what you are probably really trying to stress is that the author's reason has not been sufficiently established by evidence.

Applying the Clues

Let's look at an argument about the importance of planning and see whether we can identify descriptive and value assumptions.

> Planning is a valuable tool. Students need to be taught how to budget time and write down tasks. The best way to show college students how helpful careful planning can be for them is to require them to use a planner. Given the average course load that students take, they will have a difficult time remembering all of their assignments. Unlike high school, colleges do not have concerned adults who will remind them about assignments or ask them whether they have done their homework before they go out.

Requiring the use of a planner will help students become the goal-oriented students that every college professor wants to have in his classroom. Such a requirement will not only help students tremendously, but will also create a more successful college environment for everyone involved.

CONCLUSION   *Planning should be a requirement for students, and the best way to accomplish this goal is to require than to use a planner.*

REASONS: 1. *Students out of high school are not ready or independent enough to for classes—planning can change that.*
            2. *Students will become goal-oriented.*

First, note that the author provides no "proof" for her reasons. Thus, you might be tempted to state, "Those reasons are only assumptions; she does not know that." Wrong! They are not *assumptions!* *Remember:* identifying less-than-fully established reasons, though important, is not the same as identifying assumptions—ideas that are taken for granted as a basic part of the argument.

Now, let's see whether any descriptive assumptions can be found in the argument. Remember to keep thinking about the gap between the conclusion and the reasons as you look. First, ask yourself, "Is there any basis for believing that the reason(s) might not be true?" Then ask, "Supposing the reason(s) were true, is there any way in which the conclusion nevertheless could be false?" Try to play the role of a person who does not believe a planner should be a requirement.

Look at the two reasons. The first would be true if it were the case that the students being described are independent learners. This author is assuming that no such ability to take initiative for one's own academic success exists. How can she know such a thing? Perhaps forcing students to plan would only cause the students to have another disorderly thing to do. Thus, one descriptive assumption is that *students cannot learn to become responsible learners independently*.

Let's now suppose that the second reason is true. Planning still might not be useful to the student. Just because the author believes in the value of planning does not mean that it will change the lives or the study habits of students. Thus, an assumption connecting the first reason to the conclusion is that *students will learn how to plan and then will implement that strategy later*. This assumption also links with the second reason closely.

Consider the second reason. It is true only if the student not only absorbs the ideas of planning, but also uses them. The author is also assuming that the ideas learned through planning will then lead to a goal-oriented lifestyle. Another important assumption is that *students will change their learning styles after mastering the concepts of planning.*

Note also that there is a prescriptive quality to this essay; thus, important value assumptions underlie the reasoning. What is the author concerned about preserving? Try reverse role-playing. What would someone who disagreed with this position care about? What are the disadvantages to forcing students to plan? Your answers to these questions should lead you to the essay's value preference. For example, can you see how a preference for orderliness over independence links the reasons to the conclusion?

Avoiding Analysis of Trivial Assumptions

Writers and speakers take for granted, and should take for granted, certain self-evident things. You will want to devote your energy to evaluating important assumptions, so we want to warn you about some potential trivial assumptions. By trivial, we mean an assumption that is self-evident.

You as a reader or listener can assume that the communicator believes his reasons are true. You may want to attack the reasons as insufficient, but it is trivial to point out the writer's or speaker's assumption that the reasons are true.

Another type of trivial assumption concerns the reasoning structure. You may be tempted to state that the writer believes that the reason and conclusion are logically related. Right—but trivial. What is important is how they are logically related. It is also trivial to point out that an argument assumes that we can understand the logic, that we can understand the terminology, or that we have the appropriate background knowledge.

Avoid spending time on analyzing trivial assumptions. Your search for assumptions will be most rewarding when you locate hidden, debatable missing links.

Assumptions and Your Own Writing and Speaking

When you attempt to communicate with an audience, either by writing or speaking, you will be making numerous assumptions. Communication requires them. But, once again out of respect for your audience, you should acknowledge those assumptions, and, where possible, provide a rationale for why you are making those particular assumptions.

The logic of this approach on your part is to assist the audience in accepting your argument. You are being open and fair with them. An audience should appreciate your willingness to present your argument in its fullness.

Summary

Assumptions are ideas that, if true, enable us to claim that particular reasons provide support for a conclusion.

Clues for Discovering Descriptive Assumptions

1. Keep thinking about the gap between the conclusion and reasons.
2. Look for ideas that support reasons.
3. Identify with the opposition.
4. Recognize the potential existence of other means of attaining the advantages referred to in the reasons.
5. Learn more about the issues.

Practice Exercises

Critical Question: **What are the descriptive assumptions?**

For each of the three passages, locate important assumptions made by the author. Remember first to determine the conclusion and the reasons.

Passage 1

Everyone should consider playing poker to win money. It has gained great popularity. You can see people play on television daily, and there are many opportunities to play against real people online. This trend is an exciting opportunity for people everywhere to try and win money. Poker is simple to learn after one understands the rules and concepts behind the game. It is a game that people of all ages and experience can play!

Passage 2

Adopted children should have the right to find out who their biological parents are. They should be able to find out for personal and health reasons. Most children would want to know what happened to these people and why they were given up for adoption. Even though this meeting may not be completely the way the child had imagined it, this interaction could provide a real sense of closure for adopted children. There are people who believe that it does not matter who the biological parents are as long as the child has loving parents. It is true that having a supportive environment is necessary for children, but there will always be nagging questions for these children that will be left unanswered if they are not able to find out their biological parents. There are also health risks that can be avoided by allowing a child to find out who their parents are. A lot of diseases have hereditary links that would be useful for the child and the new family to know.

Passage 3

Recently, we have lost community members in a large fire. It only seems logical now that we start implementing fire safety presentations or courses in our schools. The last thing we want to happen is for more tragedies to occur, especially in our schools.

The fire safety training will prevent this community from losing any more lives. Educational programs provide the best way to go if we are to avoid future disasters of this type.

Sample Responses

In presenting assumptions for the following arguments, we will list only some of the assumptions being made—those which we believe are among the most significant.

Passage 1

CONCLUSION: *Everyone should play poker to win money.*

REASONS: 1. *It is a popular game.*
            2. *People of all ages and experience can play.*

In looking at the first reason, there seems to be a missing link between that reason and the conclusion. The author omits two main assumptions. One, poker is enjoyable because many people play this game. And second, that "enjoyable" means profitable. The author needs these two assumptions for him to make the jump to the idea that we should all join the poker craze.

The second reason should leave the reader wondering whether it makes sense to assume that because something can happen, it should happen. Yes, we can all certainly play poker; we can also all start forest fires, but our capacity to do so is not exactly an endorsement of the activity.

Passage 2

CONCLUSION: *Adopted children should be allowed to find their biological parents' identities.*

REASON: 1. *Knowing ones birth parents can provide many health benefits.*

(Supporting Reasons)

    a.   *Psychological closure can be achieved by finding answer to enduring questions.*

    b.   *Able to find out what their biological parents are like.*

  2. *Permits one to assess health risks.*

Try reverse role-playing, taking the position of someone who values the parents' right to privacy.

    For the first reason to be true, it must be the case that the child is bothered by not knowing their biological parentage. Surely this assumption would be true for some adopted children. Is there data that suggests a widespread burning desire to know the birth parents? If so, please present the data so we can move toward agreeing with the argument. There are many reasons to think that the child may either be satisfied not knowing or may not even be aware that he is adopted. Also, for the main reason to be enhanced by the supporting reasons, we would need to assume that meeting the biological parent would not create sharp new tensions between the individual and the adoptive parent.

CRITICAL QUESTION SUMMARY: WHY THIS QUESTION IS IMPORTANT

What Are the Descriptive Assumptions?

When you identify descriptive assumptions, you are identifying the link between a reason and the author's conclusion. If this link is flawed, the reason does not necessarily lead to the conclusion. Consequently, identifying the descriptive assumptions allows you to determine whether an author's reasons lead to a conclusion. You will want to accept a conclusion only when there are good reasons that lead to the conclusion. Thus, when you determine that the link between the reasons and conclusion is flawed, you will want to be reluctant to accept the author's conclusion.

CHAPTER

7

ARE THERE ANY FALLACIES IN THE REASONING?

Thus far, you have been working at taking the raw materials a writer or speaker gives you and assembling them into a meaningful overall structure. You have learned ways to remove the irrelevant parts from your pan as well as how to discover the "invisible glue" that holds the relevant parts together—that is, the assumptions. All these things have been achieved by asking critical questions. Let's briefly review these questions:

1. What are the issue and the conclusion?
2. What are the reasons?
3. What words or phrases are ambiguous?
4. What are the value conflicts and assumptions?
5. What are the descriptive assumptions?

Asking these questions should give you a clear understanding of the communicator's reasoning as well as a sense of where there might be strengths and weaknesses in the argument. Most remaining chapters focus on how well the structure holds up after being assembled. Your major question now is, "How acceptable is the conclusion in light of the reasons provided?" You are now ready to make your central focus *evaluation. Remember:* The objective of critical reading and listening is to judge the acceptability or worth of conclusions.

While answering our first five questions has been a necessary beginning to the evaluation process, we now move to questions requiring us to make judgments more directly and explicitly about the worth or the quality of the reasoning. Our task now is to separate the "Fools Gold" from the genuine gold. We want to isolate the best reasons—those that we want to treat most seriously.

Your first step at this stage of the evaluation process is to examine the reasoning structure to determine whether the communicator's reasoning has depended on false or highly doubtful assumptions or has "tricked" you through either a mistake in logic or other forms of deceptive reasoning. Chapter 6 focused on finding and then thinking about the quality of assumptions. This chapter, on the other hand, highlights those reasoning "tricks" that others and we call *fallacies*.

Three common tricks are:

1. providing reasoning that requires *erroneous or incorrect assumptions*;

2. *distracting us* by making information seem relevant to the conclusion when it is not; and

3. providing support for the conclusion that depends on the conclusion's already being true.

Spotting such tricks will prevent us from being unduly influenced by them. Let's see what a fallacy in reasoning looks like.

> Dear editor: I was shocked by your paper's support of Senator Spendall's arguments for a tax hike to increase state money available for improving highways. Of course the Senator favors such a hike. What else would you expect from a tax and spend liberal.

Note that the letter at first appears to be presenting a "reason" to dispute the tax-hike proposal, by citing the senator's liberal reputation. But the reason is *not relevant* to the conclusion. The question is whether the tax hike is a good idea. The letter writer has ignored the senator's reasons and has provided no specific reasons against the tax hike; instead, she has personally attacked the senator by labeling him a "tax and spend liberal." The writer has committed a fallacy in reasoning, because her argument requires an absurd assumption to be relevant to the conclusion, and shifts attention from the argument to the arguer—Senator Spendall. An unsuspecting reader not alert to this fallacy may be tricked into thinking that the writer has provided a persuasive reason.

This chapter gives you practice in identifying such fallacies so that you will not fall for such tricks.

Critical Question: **Are there any fallacies in the reasoning?**

Attention: A fallacy is a reasoning "trick" that an author might use while trying to persuade you to accept a conclusion.

A Questioning Approach to Finding Reasoning Fallacies

There are numerous reasoning fallacies. And they can be organized in many different ways. Many are so common that they have been given formal names. You can find many lengthy lists of fallacies in numerous texts and Web sites. Fortunately, you don't need to be aware of all the fallacies and their names to be able to locate them. If you ask yourself the right questions, you will be able to find reasoning fallacies—even if you can't name them.

Thus, we have adopted the strategy of emphasizing self-questioning strategies, rather than asking you to memorize an extensive list of possible kinds of fallacies. We believe, however, that knowing the names of the most common fallacies can sensitize you to fallacies and also act as a language "short cut" in communicating your reaction to faulty reasoning to others familiar with the names. Thus, we provide you with the names of fallacies as we identify the deceptive reasoning processes and encourage you to learn the names of the common fallacies described on page 98 at the end of the chapter.

We have already introduced one common fallacy to you in our Dear Editor example above. We noted that the writer personally attacked Senator Spendall instead of responding directly to the senator's reasons. Seeing such an argument, the critical thinker should immediately ask, "But what about the arguments that Senator Spendall made?" The Dear Editor reasoning illustrates the Ad Hominem fallacy. The Latin phrase Ad Hominem means "against the man or against the person." There are a variety of ways of making irrelevant attacks against a person making a claim, the most common of which is attacking his character or shifting attention to his circumstances or interests. Arguing Ad Hominem is a fallacy because the character or interests of individuals making arguments usually are not relevant to the quality of the argument being made. It is attacking the messenger instead of addressing the message.

Here is another brief example of Ad Hominem reasoning.

Sandy: "I believe that joining sororities is a waste of time and money."

Julie: "Of course you would say that, you didn't get accepted by any sorority."

Sandy: "But what about the arguments I gave to support my position?"

Julie: "Those don't count. You're just a sore loser."

You can start your list of fallacy names with this one. Here is the definition:

F: **Ad hominem:**   An attack, or an insult, on the person, rather than directly addressing the person's reasons.

Evaluating Assumptions as a Starting Point

If you have been able to locate assumptions (see Chapters 5 and 6), especially descriptive assumptions, you already possess a major skill in determining questionable assumptions and in finding fallacies. The more questionable the assumption, the less relevant the reasoning. Some "reasons," such as Ad Hominem arguments, will be so irrelevant to the conclusion that you would have to supply blatantly erroneous assumptions to provide a logical link. Such reasoning is a fallacy, and you should immediately reject it.

In the next section, we take you through some exercises in discovering other common fallacies. Once you know how to look, you will be able to find most fallacies. We suggest that you adopt the following thinking steps in locating fallacies:

1. Identify the conclusions and reasons.

2. Always keep the conclusion in mind and consider reasons that you think might be relevant to it; contrast these reasons with the author's reasons.

3. If the conclusion supports an action, determine whether the reason states a specific and/or concrete advantage or a disadvantage; if not, be wary!

4. Identify any necessary assumption by asking yourself, "If the reason were true, what would one have to believe for it to logically support the conclusion, and what does one have to believe for the reason to be true?"

5. Ask yourself, "Do these assumptions make sense?" If an obviously false assumption is being made, you have found a fallacy in reasoning, and that reasoning can then be rejected.

6. Check the possibility of being distracted from relevant reasons by phrases that strongly appeal to your emotions.

To demonstrate the process you should go through to evaluate assumptions and thus recognize many fallacies, we will examine the quality of the reasoning in the following passage. We will begin by assembling the structure.

> The question involved in this legislation is not really a question of whether alcohol consumption is or is not detrimental to health. Rather, it is a question of whether Congress is willing to have the Federal Communications Commission make an arbitrary decision that prohibits alcohol advertising on radio and television. If we should permit the FCC to take this action in regard to alcohol, what is there to prevent it from deciding next year that candy is detrimental to the public health in that it causes obesity, tooth decay, and other health problems? What about milk and eggs? Milk and eggs are high in saturated animal fat and no doubt increase the cholesterol in the bloodstream, believed by many heart specialists to be a contributing factor in heart disease. Do we want the FCC to be able to prohibit the advertising of milk, eggs, butter, and ice cream on TV?
>
> Also, we all know that no action by the federal government, however drastic, can or will be effective in eliminating alcohol consumption completely. If people want to drink alcoholic beverages, they will find some way to do so.

CONCLUSION: *The FCC should not prohibit alcohol advertising on radio and television.*

REASONS: 1. *If we permit the FCC to prohibit advertising on radio and television, the FCC will soon prohibit many kinds of advertising, because many products present potential health hazards.*
2. *No action by the federal government can or will be effective in eliminating alcohol consumption completely.*

First, we should note that both reasons refer to rather specific disadvantages of the prohibition—a good start. The acceptability of the first reason, however, depends on a hidden assumption that once we allow actions to be taken on the merits of one case, it will be impossible to stop actions on similar cases. We do not agree with this assumption, because we believe that there are plenty of steps in our legal system to prevent such actions if they appear unjustified. Thus, we judge this reason to be unacceptable. Such reasoning is an example of the *slippery slope fallacy.*

F: **Slippery Slope:**   Making the assumption that a proposed step will set off an uncontrollable chain of undesirable events, when procedures exist to prevent such a chain of events.

The relevance of the second reason is questionable because even if this reason were true, the assumption linking the reason to the conclusion—the major goal of prohibiting alcohol advertising on radio and television is to *eliminate alcohol consumption completely*—is false. A more likely goal is to *reduce consumption*. Thus we reject this reason. We call this fallacy the *searching for perfect solutions fallacy*. It takes the form: A solution to X does not deserve our support unless it destroys the problem entirely. If we ever find a perfect solution, then we should adopt it. But because the fact that part of a problem would remain after a solution is tried does not mean the solution is unwise. A particular solution may be vastly superior to no solution at all. It may move us closer to solving the problem completely.

If we waited for perfect solutions to emerge, we would often find ourselves paralyzed, unable to act. Here is another example of this fallacy: Why try to restrict people's access to abortion clinics in the United States? Even if you were successful, a woman seeking an abortion could still fly to Europe to acquire an abortion.

F: **Searching for Perfect Solution:**   Falsely assuming that because part of a problem would remain after a solution is tried, the solution should not be adopted.

Discovering Other Common Reasoning Fallacies

We are now going to take you through some exercises in discovering more common fallacies. As you encounter each exercise, try to apply the fallacy, finding hints that we listed above. Once you have developed good fallacy-detection habits, you will be able to find most fallacies. Each exercise presents some reasoning that includes fallacies. We indicate why we believe the reasoning is fallacious and then name and define the fallacy.

Exercise A

It's about time that we make marijuana an option for people in chronic severe pain. We approve drugs when society reaches a consensus about their value, and there is clearly now a consensus for such approval. A recent survey of public opinion reported that 73 percent thought medical marijuana should be allowed. In addition, the California Association for the Treatment of AIDS Victims supports smoking marijuana as a treatment option for AIDS patients.

As a first step in analyzing for fallacies, let's outline the argument.

CONCLUSION: *Smoking marijuana should be a medical option.*

REASONS: 1. *We approve drugs when a consensus of their medical value has been reached, and a recent survey shows a consensus approving marijuana as a medical treatment.*

2. *A California association supports medical marijuana use.*

First, we should note that none of the reasons points out a specific advantage of medical marijuana; thus we should be wary from the start. Next, a close look at the wording in the first reason shows a shift in meaning of a key term, and this shift tricks us. The meaning of the word consensus shifts in such a way that it looks like she has made a relevant argument when she has not. Consensus for drug approval usually means the consensus of scientific researchers about its merits, which is a very different consensus than the agreement of the American public on an opinion poll. Thus the reason fails to make sense, and we should reject it. We call this mistake in reasoning the *equivocation fallacy*. Whenever you see a key word in an argument used more than once, check to see that the meaning has not changed; if it has, be alert to the equivocation fallacy. Highly ambiguous terms or phrases are especially good candidates for the equivocation fallacy.

F: **Equivocation:**   A key word is used with two or more meanings in an argument such that the argument fails to make sense once the shifts in meaning are recognized.

Well, even if there is tricky use of the word "consensus," don't the survey results by themselves still support the conclusion? They do *only if* we accept the assumption that when something is popular, then it must be good—a mistaken assumption. The public often has not sufficiently studied a problem to provide a reasoned judgment. Be wary of appeals to common opinion or to popular sentiment. We label this mistake in reasoning the *appeal to popularity fallacy*.

F: **Appeal to Popularity (Ad populum):**   An attempt to justify a claim by appealing to sentiments that large groups of people have in common; falsely assumes that anything favored by a large group is desirable.

Now, carefully examine the author's second reason. What assumption is being made? To prove that medical marijuana is desirable, she *appeals to questionable authorities*—a California Association. A position is not good just because the authorities are for it. What is important in determining the relevance of such reasoning is the evidence that the authorities are using in making their judgment. Unless we know that these authorities have special knowledge about this issue, we must treat this reason as a fallacy. Such a fallacy is called the *Appeal to Questionable Authority fallacy*.

F: **Appeal to questionable authority:**   Supporting a conclusion by citing an authority who lacks special expertise on the issue at hand.

Now let's examine some arguments related to another controversy: Should Congress approve a federally funded child-development program that would provide day-care centers for children?

Exercise B

I am against the government's child-development program. First, I am interested in protecting the children of this country. They need to be protected from social planners and *self-righteous ideologues* who would disrupt the normal course of life and *tear them from their mothers and families* to make them *pawns* in a universal scheme designed to produce infinite happiness in 20 years. Children should grow up with their mothers, not with a series of caretakers and nurses' aides. What is at issue is whether parents shall continue to have the right to form the characters of their children, or whether the State with all its power should be given the tools and techniques for forming the young.

Let's again begin by outlining the argument.

CONCLUSION: *The government's child development program is a mistake.*

REASONS: 1. *Our children need to be protected from social planners and self-righteous ideologues, who would disrupt the normal course of life and tear them from their families.*
   2. *The parents, not the State, should have the right to form the characters of their children.*

As critical readers and listeners, we should be looking for specific facts about the program. Do you find any specifics in the first reason? No. The reason is saturated with undefined and emotionally loaded generalities. We have italicized several of these terms in the passage. Such terms will typically generate negative emotions, which the writer or speaker hopes readers and listeners will associate with the position he is attacking. The writer is engaging in name-calling and emotional appeals. The use of emotionally charged negative terms serves to distract readers and listeners from the facts.

The writer has tricked us in another way. She states that the program will "tear them from their families and mothers," and the children will be "pawns in a universal scheme." Of course, nobody wants these things to happen to their children. However, the important question is whether in fact the bill will do these things. Not likely!

The writer is playing two common tricks on us. First, she is *appealing to our emotions* with her choice of words, hoping that our emotional reactions will get us to agree with her conclusion. When communicators try to draw emotional reactions from people and then use that reaction to get them to agree to their conclusion, they commit the fallacy of an *Appeal to Emotion*. This fallacy occurs when your emotional reactions should not be relevant to the truth or falsity of a conclusion. Three of the most common places for finding this fallacy are in advertising, in political debate and in the courtroom.

Second, she has set up a position to attack which in fact does not exist, making it much easier to get us on her side. She has extended the opposition's position to an "easy-to-attack" position. The false assumption in this case is that the position attacked is the same as the position actually presented in the legislation. The lesson for the critical thinker is: When someone attacks aspects of a position, always check to see whether she is fairly representing the position. If she is not, you have located the *straw-person fallacy*.

A straw person is not real and is easy to knock down—as is the position attacked when someone commits the straw-person fallacy. The best way to check how fairly a position is being represented is to get the facts about all positions.

F: **Appeals to Emotions:**   The use of emotionally charged language to distract readers and listeners from relevant reasons and evidence.

F: **Straw Person:**   Distorting our opponent's point of view so that it is easy to attack; thus we attack a point of view that does not truly exist.

Let's now look closely at the second reason. The writer states that either parents have the right to form the characters of their children, or else the State should be given the decisive tools. For statements like this to be true, one must assume that there are only two choices. Are there? No! The writer has created a *false dilemma*. Isn't it possible for the child-development program to exist and also for the family to have a significant influence on the child? Always be cautious when controversies are treated as if only two choices are possible; there are usually more than two. When a communicator oversimplifies an issue by stating only two choices, the error is referred to as an *either-or* or *false dilemma* fallacy. To find *either-or* fallacies, be on the alert for phrases like the following:

either . . . or

the only alternative is

the two choices are

because A has not worked, only B will.

Seeing these phrases does not necessarily mean that you have located a fallacy. Sometimes there *are* only two options. These phrases are just caution signs causing you to pause and wonder: "But are there more than two options in this case?"

Can you see the false dilemma in the following interchange?

Citizen: I think that the decision by the United States to invade Iraq was a big mistake.

Politician: Why do you hate America?

F: Either-Or (Or False Dilemma):   Assuming only two alternatives when there are more than two.

The following argument contains another fallacy involving a mistaken assumption. Try to locate the assumption.

Exercise C

Student: It doesn't make sense for you to give pop quizzes to your class, Professor Jones. It just makes a lot of extra work for you and makes the students nervous. Students should not need pop quizzes to motivate them to prepare for each class.

The advice to Professor Jones requires a faulty assumption to support the conclusion. That something *should* be true—students should not need pop quizzes to motivate them to prepare for class—in no way guarantees that what *is* true will conform to the prescription. Reality, or "what is," is often in conflict with "what should be."

Another common illustration of this reasoning error occurs when discussing proposals for government regulation. For instance, someone might argue that regulating advertising for children's television programs is undesirable because parents *should* turn the channel or shut off the television if advertising is deceptive. Perhaps parents in a perfect world would behave in this fashion. Many parents, however, are too busy to monitor children's programming.

When reasoning requires us to assume incorrectly that what we think *should be* matches *what is*, or *what will be*, it commits the *wishful thinking fallacy*. We would hope that what *should* be the case would guide our behavior. Yet many observations convince us that just because advertisers, politicians, and authors should not mislead us is no protection against their regularly misleading us. The world around us is a poor imitation of what the world should be like.

Here's a final example of wishful thinking that might sound familiar to you.

> I can't wait for summer vacation time, so I can get all those books read that I've put off reading during the school year.

F: Wishful Thinking: Making the faulty assumption that because we wish X were true or false, then X is indeed true or false.

Another confusion is responsible for an error in reasoning that we often encounter when seeking explanations for behavior. A brief conversation between college roommates illustrates the confusion.

> Dan: I've noticed that Chuck has been acting really weird lately. He's acting really rude toward others and is making all kinds of messes in our residence hall and refusing to clean them up. What do you think is going on?
>
> Kevin: That doesn't surprise me. He is just a jerk.

To explain requires an analysis of why a behavior occurred. Explaining is demanding work that often tests the boundaries of what we know. In the above example, "jerkhood" is an unsatisfactory explanation of Chuck's behavior. When asked to explain why a certain behavior has occurred, it is frequently tempting to hide our ignorance of a complex sequence of causes by labeling or naming the behavior. Then we falsely assume that because we know the name, we know the cause.

We do so because the naming tricks us into believing we have identified something the person *has* or *is* that makes her act accordingly. For example, instead of specifying the complex set of internal and external factors that lead a person to manifest an angry emotion, such as problems with relationships, parental reinforcement practices, feelings of helplessness, lack of sleep, and life stressors, we say the person *has* a "bad temper" or that the person *is* hostile. Such explanations oversimplify and prevent us from seeking more insightful understanding.

The following examples should heighten your alertness to this fallacy:

1. In response to Dad's heavy drinking, Mom is asked by her adult daughter, "Why is Dad behaving so strangely?" Mom replies, "He's *having* a midlife crisis."

2. A patient cries every time the counselor asks about his childhood. An intern who watched the counseling session asks the counselor, after the patient has left, "Why does he cry when you ask about his youth?" The counselor replies, "He's neurotic."

Neither respondent satisfactorily explained what happened. For instance, the specifics of dad's genes, job pressures, marital strife, and exercise habits could have provided the basis for explaining the heavy drinking. "A midlife crisis" is not only inadequate; it misleads. We think we know why dad is drinking heavily, but we don't.

Be alert for this error when people claim that they have discovered a cause for the behavior when all they have actually done is named it.

F: **Explaining by Naming:**   Falsely assuming that because you have provided a name for some event or behavior that you have also adequately explained the event.

Looking for Diversions

Frequently, those trying to get an audience to accept some claim find that they can defend that claim by preventing the audience from taking too close a look at the relevant reasons. They prevent the close look by diversion tactics. As you look for fallacies, you will find it helpful to be especially alert to reasoning used by the communicator that *diverts your attention* from the most relevant reasons. For example, the Ad Hominem fallacy can fool us by diverting our attention too much to the nature of the person and too little to the legitimate reasons. In this section, we present exercises that illustrate other fallacies that we are likely to detect if we ask the question, "Has the author tricked us by diverting our attention?"

> Exercise D
>
> Political speech: In the upcoming election, you have the opportunity to vote for a woman who represents the future of this great nation, who has fought for democracy and defended our flag, and who has been decisive, confident, and courageous in pursuing the American Dream. This is a caring woman who has supported our children and the environment and has helped move this country toward peace, prosperity, and freedom. A vote for Goodheart is a vote for truth, vision, and common sense.

Sounds like Ms. Goodheart is a wonderful person, doesn't it? But the speech fails to provide any specifics about the senator's past record or present position on issues. Instead, it presents a series of *virtue words* that tend to be associated with deep-seated positive emotions. We call these virtue words *"Glittering Generalities,"* because they have such positive associations and are so general as to mean whatever the reader wants them to mean. The Glittering

Generality device leads us to approve or accept a conclusion without examining relevant reasons, evidence, or specific advantages or disadvantages. The Glittering Generality is much like name-calling in reverse because name-calling seeks to make us form a negative judgment without examining the evidence. The use of virtue words is a popular ploy of politicians because it serves to distract the reader or listener from specific actions or policies, which can more easily trigger disagreement.

F: **Glittering Generality:**   The use of vague emotionally appealing virtue words that dispose us to approve something without closely examining the reasons.

Let's examine another very common diversionary device.

Exercise E

I don't understand why everyone is so upset about drug companies distorting research data in order to make their pain-killer drugs seem to be less dangerous to people's health than they actually are. Taking those drugs can't be that bad. After all, there are still thousands of people using these drugs and getting pain relief from them.

What is the real issue? Is the public being misled about the safety of pain-killer drugs? But if the reader is not careful, his attention will be diverted to the issue of whether the public wants to use these drugs. When a writer or speaker shifts our attention from the issue, we can say that she has drawn a *red herring* across the trail of the original issue. Many of us are adept at committing the red herring fallacy, as the following example illustrates:

If the daughter is successful, the issue will become whether the mother is picking on her daughter, not why the daughter was out late.

You should normally have no difficulty spotting red herrings as long as you keep the real issue in mind as well as the kind of evidence needed to resolve it.

F: **Red Herring:**   An irrelevant topic is presented to divert attention from the original issue and help to "win" an argument by shifting attention away from the argument and to another issue. The fallacy sequence in this instance is as follows: (a) Topic A is being discussed; (b) Topic B is introduced as though it is relevant to topic A, but it is not; and (c) Topic A is abandoned.

This sort of "reasoning" is fallacious because merely changing the topic of discussion hardly counts as an argument against a claim.

Sleight of Hand: Begging the Question

Our last illustrated fallacy is a particularly deceptive one. Sometimes a conclusion is supported by itself; only the words have been changed to fool the innocent! For example, to argue that dropping out of school is *undesirable* because it is *bad* is to argue not at all. The conclusion is "proven" by the conclusion (in different words). Such an argument *begs the question*, rather than answering it. Let's look at an example that is a little less obvious.

> Programmed learning texts are clearly superior to traditional texts in learning effectiveness because it is highly advantageous for learning to have materials presented in a step-by-step fashion.

Again, the reason supporting the conclusion restates the conclusion in different words. By definition, programmed learning is a step-by-step procedure. The writer is arguing that such a procedure is good because it is good. A legitimate reason would be one that points out a specific advantage to programmed learning such as greater retention of learned material.

Whenever a conclusion is *assumed* in the reasoning when it should have been proven, begging the question has occurred. When you outline the structure of an argument, check the reasons to be sure that they do not simply repeat the conclusion in different words and check to see that the conclusion is not used to prove the reasons. In case you are confused, let's illustrate with two examples, one argument that begs the question and one that does not.

> (1) To allow the press to keep their sources confidential is very advantageous to the country because it increases the likelihood that individuals will report evidence against powerful people.

> (2) To allow the press to keep their sources confidential is very advantageous to the country because it is highly conducive to the interests of the larger community that private individuals should have the privilege of providing information to the press without being identified.

Paragraph (2) begs the question by basically repeating the conclusion. It fails to point out what the specific advantages are and simply repeats that confidentiality of sources is socially used.

F: **Begging the Question:** An argument in which the conclusion is assumed in the reasoning.

USING THIS CRITICAL QUESTION

When you spot a fallacy, you have found a legitimate basis for rejecting the argument. But in the spirit of constructive critical thinking, you want to continue the discussion of the issue. Unfortunately, the author of a book or article is unavailable for more conversation. But in those instances where the fallacy occurred in an oral argument, your best bet for an enduring conversation is to ask the person who committed the fallacy if there is not a better reason for the conclusion. For example, if a red herring fallacy occurs, ask the speaker if it would be possible to return to the original issue.

Summary of Reasoning Errors

We have taken you through exercises that illustrate a number of ways in which reasoning may be faulty. We have not listed all the ways, but we have given you a good start. We have saved some additional fallacies for later chapters because you are most likely to spot them when you focus on the particular question central to that chapter. As you encounter each additional fallacy, be sure to add it to your fallacy list.

To find reasoning fallacies, keep in mind what kinds of reasons are good reasons—that is, the evidence and the moral principles relevant to the issue. Reasoning should be *rejected* whenever you have found mistaken assumptions, distractions, or support for the conclusion that already assumes the truth of the conclusion. Reasoning should be *approached cautiously* when it appeals to group-approved attitudes and to authority. You should always ask, "Are there good reasons to consider such appeals as persuasive evidence?" A precautionary note is in order here: Do not automatically reject reasoning that relies on appeals to authority or group-approved attitudes. Carefully evaluate such reasoning. For example, if most physicians in the country choose to take up jogging, that information is important to consider in deciding whether jogging is beneficial. Some authorities do possess valuable information. Because of their importance as a source of evidence, we discuss appeals to authority in detail in the next chapter.

Clues for Locating and Assessing Fallacies in Reasoning

You should reject reasoning when the author:

- attacks a person or a person's background, instead of the person's ideas
- uses slippery slope reasoning
- reflects a search for perfect solutions
- equivocates
- inappropriately appeals to common opinion
- appeals to questionable authority
- appeals to emotions
- attacks a straw person
- presents a faulty dilemma
- engages in wishful thinking
- explains by naming
- diverts attention from the issue
- distracts with glittering generalities
- begs the question

Expanding Your Knowledge of Fallacies

We recommend that you consult texts and some web sites to expand your awareness and understanding of reasoning fallacies. Damer's *Attacking Faulty Reasoning* is a good source to help you become more familiar with reasoning fallacies. There are dozens of fallacy lists on the web, which vary greatly in quality. A few of the more helpful sites, which provide descriptions and examples of numerous fallacies, are listed below:

> The Nizkor Project: Fallacies. http://www.nizkor.org/features/fallacies/
>
> The Fallacy Zoo, by Brian Yoder: (list of basic fallacies with examples) *http://www.goodart.org/fallazoo.htm*
>
> The Fallacy Files by Gary Curtis http://www.fallacyfiles.org/
>
> Stephen's Guide to the Logical Fallacies http://www.datanation.com/fallacies/

Fallacies and Your Own Writing and Speaking

When you communicate, you necessarily engage in reasoning. If your purpose is to present a well-reasoned argument, in which you do not want to "trick" the reader into agreeing with you, then you will want to avoid committing reasoning fallacies. Awareness of possible errors committed by writers provides you with warnings to heed when you construct your own arguments. You can avoid fallacies by checking your own assumptions very carefully, by remembering that most controversial issues require you to get specific about advantages and disadvantages, and by keeping a checklist handy of possible reasoning fallacies.

Practice Exercises

Critical Question: **Are there any fallacies in the reasoning?**

Try to identify fallacies in the reasoning in each of the three practice passages.

Passage 1

The surgeon general has overstepped his bounds by recommending that explicit sex education begin as early as third grade. It is obvious that he is yet another victim of the AIDS hysteria sweeping the nation. Unfortunately, his media-influenced announcement has given new life to those who favor explicit sex education—even to the detriment of the nation's children.

Sexuality has always been a topic of conversation reserved for the family. Only recently has sex education been forced on young children. The surgeon general's recommendation removes the role of the family entirely. It should be up to parents to explain sex to their children in a manner with which they are comfortable. Sex education exclusive of the family is stripped of values or any sense of morality, and should thus be discouraged. For years families have taken the responsibility of sex education, and that's the way it should remain.

Sex education in schools encourages experimentation. Kids are curious. Letting them in on the secret of sex at such a young age will promote blatant promiscuity. Frank discussions of sex are embarrassing for children, and they destroy the natural modesty of girls.

Passage 2

Sandra: I don't see why you are so against permitting beer to be sold at the new University Student Union. After all, a survey of our students shows that 80 percent are in favor of the proposal.

Joe: Of course, you will be in favor of serving any alcoholic beverage at any time anywhere. You are one of the biggest alcoholics on our campus.

Passage 3

Bill: Countries that harbor terrorists who want to destroy the United States must be considered enemies of the United States. Any country that does not relinquish terrorists to the American justice system is clearly on the side of the terrorists. This sort of action means that the leaders of these countries do not wish to see justice done to the terrorists and care more about hiding murderers, rapists, thieves, and anti-democrats.

Taylor: That's exactly the kind of argument that I would expect from someone who has relatives who have worked for the CIA. But it seems to me that once you start labeling countries that disagree with America on policy as enemies, then eventually almost all countries will be considered our enemies, and we will be left with no allies.

Bill: If that's the case, too bad. America stands for freedom, for democracy, and for truth. So it can stand against the world. Besides, the United States should be able to convince countries hostile to the United States of the error of their ways because our beliefs have a strong religious foundation.

Taylor: Do you really think most religious people are in favor of war? A Gallup poll last week found that 75 percent of highly religious people didn't think we should go to war with countries harboring terrorists.

Bill: I think that's an overestimate. How many people did they survey?

Taylor: I'm not sure. But getting back to your original issue, the biggest problem with a tough stand against countries that harbor terrorists is that such a policy is not going to wipe out terrorism in the world.

Bill: Why do you keep defending the terrorists? I thought you were a patriot. Besides, this is a democracy, and most Americans agree with me.

Sample Responses

Passage 1

CONCLUSION: *Sex education should not be taught in schools.*

REASONS: 1. *The Surgeon General's report reflects hysteria.*
          2. *The report removes the role of the family entirely.*
          3. *It is the job of parents.*
          4. *Education encourages promiscuity.*

The author begins the argument by attacking the surgeon general rather than the issue. She claims that the recommendation is a by-product of the AIDS hysteria rather than extensive research. Her suggestion that the surgeon general issues reports in reaction to hot topics in the media undermines his credibility and character and is therefore *ad hominem.*

The second paragraph is a straw-person fallacy because it implies that the goal of sex education is to supply all the child's sex education.

Her third reason confuses "what is" with "what should be." Just because sex education *should be* up to the parents does not mean that they *will* provide education.

The fourth reason presents a false dilemma—either keep sex education out of the schools or face morally loose, value-free children. But isn't it possible to have morally loose children even when sex education is taking place in the home? Isn't it also a possibility that both parents and the schools can play a role in sex education? Might not education result in children who are prepared to handle the issue of sex in their lives rather than morally deficient delinquents?

Passage 2

SANDRA'S CONCLUSION: *Beer should be served at the University Union.*

SANDRA'S REASON: *Most students are in favor of the idea.*

JOE'S CONCLUSION: *Beer should not be served in the University Union* (implied).

JOE'S REASON: *We should not listen to Sandra's argument because she is an alcoholic.*

Both Sandra and Joe commit fallacies in their arguments. Sandra bases her claim about the desirability of beer in the Union on the majority view of students that beer should be served. She makes the erroneous assumption that if the majority favors an action, the action is proper. Students might be for the proposal, but they also may have given little thought to the advantages and disadvantages of making beer more easily available.

Joe commits two fallacies in his tiny argument. First, he attacks Sandra, rather than addressing Sandra's reasoning. Sandra's alleged alcoholism is not the issue. She provides a reason for her support for beer in the Union; Joe ignores that reason and attacks her instead. Second, Joe responds to a straw man argument when he responds to Sandra by extending what she did say to an extreme position that she did not take in her statement. Nowhere in her argument did Sandra favor drinking with no restrictions.

CRITICAL QUESTION SUMMARY: WHY THIS QUESTION IS IMPORTANT

Are there Any Fallacies in the Reasoning?

Once you have identified the reasons, you want to determine whether the author used any reasoning tricks, or fallacies. If you identify a fallacy in reasoning, that reason does not provide good support for the conclusion. Consequently, you would not want to accept an author's conclusion on the basis of that reason. If the author provides no good reasons, you would not want to accept her conclusion. Thus, looking for fallacies in reasoning is another important step in determining whether you will accept or reject the author's conclusion.

How Good Is the Evidence: Intuition, Personal Experience, Testimonials, and Appeals to Authority?

In the last chapter, you made major inroads into the process of evaluating persuasive communications by learning how to detect some fallacies in reasoning. In the following chapters, we continue our focus on evaluation as we learn to ask critical questions about a specific part of the reasoning structure: claims about the "facts." Let's see what such claims look like.

> Practicing yoga reduces the risk of cancer.
>
> Playing video games increases hand-eye coordination.
>
> Microwaves are not safe; *Time* magazine reports that microwave-related injuries have increased by 23 percent over the last year.

What do we make of these claims? Are they legitimate? Most reasoning includes claims such as these. In this chapter, we begin the process of evaluating such claims.

(?) *Critical Question:* **How good is the evidence: intuition, personal experience, testimonials, and appeals to authority?**

The Need for Evidence

Almost all reasoning we encounter includes beliefs about the way the world is,
was, or is going to be that the communicator wants us to accept as "facts."
These beliefs can be conclusions, reasons, or assumptions. We can refer to
such beliefs as *factual claims.*

The first question you should ask about a factual claim is, "*Why should I
believe it?*"

Your next question is, "*Does the claim need evidence to support it?*" If it does,
and if there is no evidence, the claim is a *mere assertion.* You should seriously
question the dependability of mere assertions!

If there is evidence, your next question is, "*How good is the evidence?*"

To evaluate reasoning, we need to remember that some factual claims
can be counted on more than others. For example, you probably feel quite
certain that the claim "most United States senators are men" is true, but less
certain that the assertion "practicing yoga reduces the risk of cancer" is true.

Because it is extremely difficult, if not impossible, to establish the *absolute*
truth or falsity of most claims, rather than ask whether they are *true*, we prefer
to ask whether they are *dependable.* In essence, we want to ask, "*Can we count on
such beliefs?*" The greater the quality and quantity of evidence supporting a
claim, the more we can *depend on it,* and the more we can call the claim a "*fact.*"

For example, abundant evidence exists that George Washington was the
first president of the United States of America. Thus, we can treat that claim
as a fact. On the other hand, there is much conflicting evidence for the belief
"alcoholism is a disease." We thus can't treat this belief as a fact. The major difference between claims that are *opinions* and those that are *facts* is the present
state of the relevant evidence. The more supporting evidence there is for a
belief, the more "factual" the belief becomes.

Before we judge the persuasiveness of a communication, we need to
know which factual claims are most dependable. How do we determine
dependability? We ask questions like the following:

What is your proof?	How do you know that's true?
Where's the evidence?	Why do you believe that?
Are you sure that's true?	Can you prove it?

You will be well on your way to being among the best critical thinkers when you develop the habit of regularly asking these questions. They require those making arguments to be responsible by revealing the basis for their arguments. Anyone with an argument that you should consider will not hesitate to answer these questions. They know they have substantial support for their claims and, consequently, will want to share their evidence in the hope that you will learn to share their conclusions. When people react to simple requests for evidence with anger or withdrawal, they usually do so because they are embarrassed as they realize that, without evidence, they should have been less assertive about their beliefs.

When we regularly ask these questions, we notice that for many beliefs there is insufficient evidence to clearly support or refute them. For example, much evidence supports the assertion that taking an aspirin every other day reduces the risk of heart attack, although some other evidence disputes it. In such cases, we need to make judgments about where the *preponderance of evidence* lies as we decide on the dependability of the factual claim.

Making such judgments requires us to ask the important question, "*How good is the evidence?*" The next three chapters focus on questions we need to ask to decide how well communicators have supported their factual claims. The more dependable the factual claims, the more persuasive the communications should be.

Locating Factual Claims

We encounter factual claims as (a) *descriptive conclusions*, (b) *reasons* used to support either descriptive or prescriptive conclusions, or (c) *descriptive assumptions*. Let's examine an example of each within brief arguments.

> (a) *Frequent use of headphones may cause hearing loss.* Researchers studied the frequency and duration of head phone use among 251 college students and found that 49 percent of the students showed evidence of hearing impairment.

Note that "frequent headphone use may cause hearing loss" is a factual claim that is a descriptive conclusion supported by research evidence. In this case, we want to ask, "Is that conclusion—a factual claim—justified by the evidence?"

> (b) This country needs tougher gun regulations. *Recent crime statistics report an increase in the number of gun related crimes over the last 10 years.*

Note that the factual claim here is the statistic reporting "*an increase in the number of gun-related crimes over the last 10 years*," and it functions as a reason supporting a prescriptive conclusion. In this case, we want to ask, "Is that reason—a factual claim—justified by the evidence?"

> (c) Our country needs to decrease its dependency on fossil fuels. Although hybrid cars are expensive, they are an excellent means to lower gas and oil consumption in America. Also, our government needs to pursue alternative energy sources at all costs because our oil dependency is leading our country to unfavorable international actions. (Unstated descriptive assumption linking the reasons to the conclusion: *The monetary costs of switching to hybrid cars and alternative energy sources are far less than the political benefits to decreasing dependency on fossil fuels.*)

This factual claim is a descriptive assumption, which may or may not be dependable. Before we believe the assumption, and thus the reason, we want to ask, "How well does evidence support the assumption?" You will find that while many communicators perceive the desirability of supporting their reasons with evidence, they don't see the need to make their assumptions explicit. Thus, evidence for assumptions is rarely presented, even though in many cases such evidence would be quite helpful in deciding the quality of an argument.

Sources of Evidence

When should we accept a factual claim as dependable? There are three instances in which we will be most inclined to agree with a factual claim:

1. when the claim appears to be undisputed common knowledge, such as the claim "weight lifting increases muscular body mass;"
2. when the claim is the conclusion from a well-reasoned argument;
3. when the claim is adequately supported by solid evidence in the same communication or by other evidence that we know.

Our concern in this chapter is the third instance. Determining the adequacy of evidence requires us to ask, "How good is the evidence?" To answer this question, we must first ask, "What do we mean by *evidence?*"

 Attention: Evidence is explicit information shared by the communicator that is used to back up or to justify the dependability of a factual claim (see Chapter 3). In prescriptive arguments, evidence will be needed to support reasons that are factual claims; in descriptive arguments, evidence will be needed to directly support a descriptive conclusion.

The quality of evidence depends on the kind of evidence it is. Thus, to evaluate evidence, we first need to ask, "What kind of evidence is it?" Knowing the kind of evidence tells us what questions we should ask.

Major kinds of evidence include:

- intuition
- personal experience
- testimonials
- appeals to authorities
- personal observations
- case examples
- research studies
- analogies.

When used appropriately, each kind of evidence can be "good evidence." It can help support an author's claim. Like a gold prospector closely examining the gravel in her pan for potentially high-quality ore, we must closely examine the evidence to determine its quality. We want to know, "Does an author's evidence provide dependable support for her claim?" Thus, we begin to evaluate evidence by asking, "*How good is the evidence?*" Always keep in the back of your mind that no evidence will be a slam dunk that gets the job done conclusively. You are looking for better evidence; searching for altogether wonderful evidence will be frustrating.

In this chapter and the next one, we examine what kinds of questions we can ask of each kind of evidence to help us decide. Kinds of evidence examined in this chapter are intuition, authority, and testimonials.

Intuition as Evidence

When we use intuition to support a claim, we rely on "common sense," or on our "gut feelings," or on hunches. When a communicator supports a claim by saying "common sense tells us" or "I just know that it's true," she is using intuition as her evidence.

A major problem with intuition is that it is private; others have no way to judge its dependability. Thus, when intuitive beliefs differ, as they so often do, we have no solid basis for deciding which ones to believe. Also, much intuition relies on unconscious processing that largely ignores relevant evidence and reflects strong biases. Consequently, we must be very wary of claims backed up only by intuition.

However, sometimes "intuition" may in fact be relying on some other kind of evidence, such as extensive relevant personal experiences and readings. For example, when an experienced pilot has an intuition that the plane doesn't feel right as it taxis for takeoff, we might be quite supportive of further safety checks of the plane prior to takeoff. Sometimes "hunches" are not blind. As critical thinkers, we would want to find out whether claims relying on intuition have any other kinds of evidential support.

Dangers of Appealing to Personal Experience as Evidence

The following arguments use a particular kind of evidence to support a factual claim.

> "I cross the street all the time without looking, and I have never been hit by a car. Therefore I do not see the need to look both ways before crossing."

> "I always feel better after having a big slice of chocolate cake, so I think that anyone who is depressed just needs to eat more chocolate cake."

Both arguments appeal to personal experiences as evidence. Phrases like "I know someone who . . . ," and "In my experience, I've found . . ." should alert you to such evidence. Because personal experiences are very vivid in our memories, we often rely on them as evidence to support a belief. For example, you might have a really frustrating experience with a car mechanic because she greatly overcharges you for her services, leading you to believe that most car mechanics overcharge. While the generalization about car mechanics may or may not be true, relying on such experiences as the basis for a general belief is a mistake! Because a single personal experience, or even an accumulation of personal experiences, is not enough to give you a *representative* sample of experiences, personal experiences often lead us to commit the Hasty Generalization fallacy. A single striking experience or several such experiences can demonstrate that certain outcomes are *possible*; for example, you may have met several people who claim their lives were saved because they were not wearing their seat belts when they got into a car accident. Such experiences, however, cannot demonstrate that such outcomes are *typical* or *probable*.

F: **Hasty Generalization Fallacy:**   A person draws a conclusion about a large group based on experiences with only a few members of the group.

We will revisit this fallacy in Chapter 9 when we discuss research evidence and issues of sampling.

Personal Testimonials as Evidence

I saw a note on a service station wall stating:

"Jane did a wonderful job fixing the oil leak my car had. You should always take your car to Jane to fix that engine problem you have."

This book looks great. On the back cover comments from readers say, "I could not put this book down."

"All my friends are saying about the new toothpaste. I should buy same quality."

Commercials, ads for movies, recommendations on the backs of book jackets, and "proofs" of the existence of the paranormal or other controversial or extraordinary life events often try to persuade by using a special kind of appeal to personal experience; they quote particular persons as saying that a given idea or product is good or bad, or that extraordinary events have occurred, based upon their personal experiences. Such quoted statements serve as *personal testimonials*. You may have listened to personal testimonials from college students when you chose your college.

How helpful is such evidence? Usually, it is not very helpful at all. In most cases, we should pay little attention to personal testimonials until we find out much more about the expertise, interests, values, and biases behind them. We should be especially wary of each of the following problems with testimonials:

- **Selectivity.** People's experiences differ greatly. Those trying to persuade us have usually carefully selected the testimony they use. We should always ask the question, "What was the experience like for those whom we have not heard from?" Also, the people who provide the testimonials have often been selective in their attention, paying special attention to information that confirms their beliefs and ignoring disconfirming information. Often, believing is seeing! Our *expectancies* greatly influence how we experience events. If we believe that aliens live among us, or that humans never really landed on the moon, then we are more likely to see ambiguous images as aliens or as proof of the government conspiracy regarding the moon landing.

- **Personal interest.** Many testimonials such as those used for books, movies, and television products come from people who have something to gain from their testimony. For example, drug companies often give doctors grants to do research, as long as they prescribe the drug company's brands of medication. Thus, we need to ask, "Does the person providing the testimony have a relationship with what he is advocating such that we can expect a strong bias in his testimony?"

- **Omitted information.** Testimonials rarely provide sufficient information about the basis for the judgment. For example, when a friend of yours encourages you to go see this new movie because it is the "best movie ever," you should ask, with warmth, about what makes the movie so impressive. Our standards for judgment may well differ from the standards of those giving the testimony. We often have too little information to decide whether we should treat such claims seriously.

- **The human factor.** One reason that testimonials are so convincing is that they come from human beings and they are very vivid and detailed, a marked contrast to statistics and graphs, which tend to be very abstract. They are often provided by very enthusiastic people, who seem trustworthy, well-meaning, and honest. Such people make us *want* to believe them.

Appeals to Authority as Evidence

> "According to my doctor, recent studies have shown that eating a couple of teaspoons of sugar a day can help fight the common cold."

The speaker has defended her claim by appealing to authority—sources that are supposed to know more than most of us about a given topic—so-called experts. When communicators appeal to authorities or experts, they appeal to people who they believe are in a position to have access to certain facts and to have special qualifications for drawing conclusions from the facts. You encounter appeals to many forms of authority on a daily basis. And you have little choice but to rely on them because you have neither the time nor the knowledge to become adept in more than a few dimensions of our very complicated lives.

> Movie reviewers: "One of the ten best movies of the year." Valerie Viewer, *Toledo Gazette.*
>
> Organizations: "The American Medical Association supports this position."
>
> Researchers: "Studies show . . ."
>
> Relatives: "My grandfather says . . ."
>
> Religion: "The Koran says . . ."

Magazines: "According to *Newsweek* . . ."

College professors: "The appropriate interpretation of Plato is . . ."

Expert witnesses: "It is my belief that the defendant . . ."

You can easily add to our list. It should be obvious that some appeals to authority should be taken much more seriously as evidence than others. Why? Some authorities are much more careful in giving an opinion than others. For example, *Newsweek* and *Time* are much more likely to carefully evaluate the available evidence prior to stating an opinion than is *The National Enquirer*. Articles on schizophrenia are more likely to be based on carefully collected evidence if they are posted on the National Institute of Mental Health Web site than if they are posted on a personal Web page. Our relatives are much less likely than editorial writers for major newspapers to have systematically evaluated a political candidate.

You should remember, that for many reasons, *authorities are often wrong*. Also, they often disagree. The following examples, taken from *The Experts Speak*, are clear reminders of the fallibility of expert opinion (Christopher Cerf and Victor Navasky, 1998, Rev. Ed., Villard Books, New York).

"It is once and for all clear. . . that the earth is in the middle of the world and all weights move towards it." Ptolemy, *The Almagest*, second century A.D., p. 5.

"Nature intended women to be our slaves . . . They are our property . . . They belong to us, just as a tree that bears fruit belongs to a gardener. What a mad idea to demand equality for women! . . . Women are nothing but machines for producing children." Napoleon Bonaparte (1769–1821), p. 32.

"Video won't be able to hold onto any market it captures after the first six months. People will soon get tired of staring at a plywood box every night." Darryl F. Zanuck (Head of Twentieth Century Fox Studios), ca. 1946, p. 41.

"If excessive smoking actually plays a role in the production of lung cancer, it seems to be a minor one." Dr. W. C. Heuper (National Cancer Institute), quoted in *The New York Times*, April 14, 1954, p. 228.

These quotes should remind us that we need to ask critical questions when communicators appeal to authority. We need to ask, "*Why should we believe this authority?*" More specifically, we should ask the following questions of authorities.

How much expertise or training does the authority have about the subject about which he is communicating? Is this a topic the person has studied for a long time? Or, has the person had extensive experience related to the topic?

Was the authority in a position to have especially good access to pertinent facts? For example, was she a firsthand observer of the events about which she makes claims? Or, has a newspaper reporter, for example, actually witnessed an event, or has she merely relied upon reports from others? If the authority is not a firsthand observer, whose claims is she repeating? Why should we rely on those claims? In general, you should be more impressed by *primary sources*—or direct observers— than by *secondary sources*, those who are relying on others for their evidence. *Time* and *Newsweek*, for example, are secondary sources, while research journals such as the *Journal of the American Medical Association* are primary sources.

Is there good reason to believe that the authority is relatively free of distorting influences? Among the factors that can influence how evidence is reported are personal needs, prior expectations, general beliefs, attitudes, values, theories, and ideologies. These can subconsciously or deliberately affect how evidence is presented. For example, if a public university president is asked whether cuts in funding for education are bad for the university, he will in all probability answer "yes" and give a number of good reasons. He may be giving an unbiased view of the situation. Because of his position, however, we would want to be concerned about the possibility that he has sought out only those reasons that justify his own biases.

By having bias and prejudice, we mean the existence of a strong personal feeling about the goodness or badness of something up front before we look at the evidence, such that it interferes with our ability to evaluate evidence fairly. Because many factors bias us in virtually all our judgments, we cannot expect any authority to be *totally* unbiased. We can, however, expect less bias from some authorities than from others and try to determine such bias by seeking information about the authority's personal interest in the topic. For example, we want to be especially wary when an authority stands to benefit financially from the actions she advocates.

Because an authority can have a personal interest in an issue and still make dependable claims, we should not reject a claim simply because we suspect that the authority's personal interests may interfere with her fairness. One helpful step we can take is to check to see whether authorities with diverse attitudes, prior expectations, values, and interests agree. Thus we need to ask the questions: *"Has the authority developed a reputation for frequently making dependable claims? Have we been able to rely on this authority in the past?"*

You will want to be especially concerned about the quality of authorities when you encounter factual claims on the Internet. When we go on-line, virtually everyone becomes an "authority," because people are free to claim whatever they wish, and there is no built-in process to evaluate such claims. It is clearly a "buyers beware" situation!

USING THIS CRITICAL QUESTION

When you identify problems with intuition, personal experience, testimonials, and appeals to authority as evidence, you then have a proper basis for hesitating to accept the conclusion based on that evidence. Knowing these problems gives you some protection against bogus reasoning. However, you do want to work hard to be fair to the arguments that people present for your consideration. So it makes sense to ask those who provide you with insubstantial evidence whether they can give you some better evidence. Give arguments every chance they deserve.

Summary

> ### Clues for Evaluating the Evidence
>
> Use the following questions to help assess the various kinds of evidence.
>
> #### Intuition
> ? Does the intuition have any other kind of evidential support?
>
> #### Authority
> ? How much expertise or training does the authority have on this particular subject?
>
> ? Was the authority in a position to have especially good access to pertinent facts?
>
> ? Is there good reason to believe that the authority is relatively free of distorting influences?
>
> ? Has the authority developed a reputation for frequently making dependable claims?
>
> ? Have we been able to rely on this authority in the past?
>
> #### Personal Testimony
> ? What biases or interests might be affecting the person's testimony?
>
> ? Does the person have any expertise to assist his or her judgment?
>
> ? How do the person's value assumptions affect his or her testimony?
>
> ? Whose personal testimony might be helpful in assessing this person's testimony?
>
> ? What information has been left out in this personal testimony?

In this chapter, we have focused on the evaluation of several kinds of evidence used to support factual claims: intuition, personal experience, personal testimonials, and appeals to authorities. Such evidence must be relied on with caution. We have provided you with some questions you should ask to determine whether such evidence is *good evidence*. In the next chapter, we discuss other kinds of evidence, as we continue to ask the question, "*How good is the evidence?*"

Practice Exercises

 Critical Question: **How good is the evidence: intuition, personal experience, testimonials, and appeals to authority?**

Evaluate the evidence in the following three passages.

Passage 1

Consumers are constantly being cheated by big corporations and marketing departments. People are finding themselves paying more and more for the same product just so the corporation can make more money. To make matters worse, big corporations work with their marketing departments to find ways to make their products desirable, while not actually increasing the quality of the product.

Consumers are angry about being cheated and they are clamoring for a change. A recent survey elicited the following comments:

Michelle K., mother: "It seems that every time I open a bag of potato chips there is more air then chips. I remember when the bag used to be mostly full. Now you are lucky to get a bag a third full of chips. Not to mention the price! When will these things stop costing so much?"

George Z., truck driver: "I like nothing better than eating a box of crackers and drinking pop while on the road. Yet, every time I am in the store buying more snacks I feel like I am spending a fortune. How much can it possibly cost to make crackers and pop?"

Sarah L., attorney: "The price of bread has risen substantially over the last 12 years. Every year the price has gone up, and yet it is the same old bread. The bread manufacturers have done absolutely nothing to increase the quality of the bread, but the price is still rising. The bread does not last longer. It is not softer. Yet, the price is still rising! Someone should sue the bread manufacturers."

Passage 2

Are Botox injections a safe alternative to face lifts? According to an interview with Dr. N.O. Worries published in *Cosmo*, there are no dangerous side effects associated with Botox injections. Dr. Worries performs hundreds of Botox injections each month, is well established as a physician in New York City, and has her own private practice. She claims she has never had a serious problem with any of her injections, and her patients have never reported side effects. Furthermore, Hollywood's Association for Cosmetic Surgeons officially stated in a press release that Botox has never been shown to cause any negative effects, despite what other physicians might argue.

Passage 3

Are Macs really better than PCs? The answer is a resounding yes! *Computer Nerds Quarterly* recently ran an article thoroughly outlining every advantage that Macs have over PCs. Furthermore, just ask Mac users and they will quickly explain how Macs are superior to PCs. For example, Sherry, a Mac user, states, "My Mac is the best thing I ever purchased. It is fast and easy to use. Plus, it has never crashed on me. All of my friends who have PCs have complained about all kinds of problems my Mac has never had." More importantly, a recent report in *Consumer Affairs* states that more new businesses are using Mac based systems than PC based systems. Clearly, Macs are a cut above the PCs.

Sample Responses

Passage 1

CONCLUSION: *Consumers are angry at big corporations because of rising prices of their products without an increase in quality.*

REASON: *Three people had voiced their dissatisfaction with rising prices and corporate practices.*

Although the general conclusion may or may not be accurate, we should not rely on these testimonials as good "proof." This passage illustrates well the weaknesses of testimony as evidence. How typical are these "horror stories"? Would other consumers have voiced no complaint about products' prices? How were the interviews conducted? Is the author's selection of interview comments biased? Did the individuals know what the interviewer was trying to prove and thus try to please the interviewer? Have prices of other products remained constant while some have risen? Before we conclude that consumers are being cheated by big corporations, we would want much better evidence than just a few testimonials. What the testimonials do tell us, however, is that it is possible for consumers to be upset about the cost of certain products.

Passage 2

CONCLUSION: *Botox injections are safe.*

REASON: *A cosmetic surgeon and a state professional organization claim Botox is safe.*

How much should we depend on these appeals to authority? Not much. First, both authorities are likely to be very biased. They stand to gain financially by making safety claims. Dr. Worries' testimony is especially suspect because it is based on her experiences only. She has probably not sought out evidence of failures. The claims of the professional organization are as questionable as those of Dr. Worries because the organization is comprised of cosmetic surgeons, who probably perform Botox injections. If the organization were to have offered some sort of systematic research for why Botox is safe, perhaps its claims would be less suspect.

How Good is the Evidence: Personal Observation, Research Studies, Case Examples, and Analogies?

In this chapter, we continue our evaluation of evidence. We focus on four common kinds of evidence: personal observation, research studies, case examples, and analogies. We need to question each of these when we encounter them as evidence.

 Critical Question: **How good is the evidence: personal observation, research studies, case examples, and analogies?**

Personal Observation

One valuable kind of evidence is personal observation, the basis for much scientific research. For example, we feel confident of something we actually see. Thus, we tend to rely on eyewitness testimony as evidence. A difficulty with personal observation, however, is the tendency to see or hear what we wish to see or hear, selecting and remembering those aspects of an experience that are most consistent with our previous experience and background.

Observers, unlike certain mirrors, do not give us "pure" observations. What we "see" and report is filtered through a set of values, biases, attitudes, and expectations. Because of such influences, observers often disagree about what they perceive. Thus, we should be wary of reliance on observations made by any single observer in situations in which we might expect observations among observers to vary.

Three illustrations should help you see the danger of relying on personal observation as evidence:

- A player says he crossed the end zone and the referee says the player stepped out of bounds first.
- There is a car accident at a busy intersection. The drivers blame each other. Witnesses alternately blame the drivers and a third car that sped off.
- You send what you believe to be a friendly e-mail to a friend. Your friend responds to you wanting to know why you sent such a mean note to her.

While personal observations can often be valuable sources of evidence, we need to recognize that they are not unbiased "mirrors of reality"; and when they are used to support controversial conclusions, we should seek verification by other observers as well as other kinds of evidence to support the conclusion. For example, if an employee complains that certain remarks made by her boss are discriminatory, the claim is more credible if others who heard the remarks also think the comments were discriminatory. Also, remember that observational reports get increasingly problematic as the time between the observation and the report of the observation increases.

When reports of observations in newspapers, magazines, books, television, and the Internet are used as evidence, you need to determine whether there are good reasons to rely on such reports. The most reliable reports will be based on recent observations made by several people observing under optimal conditions who have no apparent, strong expectations or biases related to the event being observed.

Research Studies as Evidence

"Studies show . . ."

"Research investigators have found in a recent survey that . . ."

"A report in the *New England Journal of Medicine* indicates . . ."

One form of authority that relies a great deal on observation and often carries special weight is the research study: usually a systematic collection of observations by people trained to do scientific research. How dependable are research findings? Like appeals to any authority, we cannot tell about the dependability of research findings until we ask lots of questions.

Society has turned to the scientific method as an important guide for determining the facts because the relationships among events in our world are very complex, and because humans are fallible in their observations and theories about these events. The scientific method attempts to avoid many of the built-in biases in our observations of the world and in our intuition and common sense.

What is special about the scientific method? Above all, it seeks information in the form of *publicly verifiable data*—that is, data obtained under conditions such that other qualified people can make similar observations and see whether they get the same results. Thus, for example, if one researcher reports that she was able to achieve cold fusion in she lab, the experiment would seem more credible if other researchers could obtain the same results.

A second major characteristic of scientific method is *control*—that is, the using of special procedures to reduce error in observations and in the interpretation of research findings. For example, if bias in observations may be a major problem, researchers might try to control this kind of error by using multiple observers to see how well they agree with one another. Physical scientists frequently maximize control by studying problems in the laboratory so that they can minimize extraneous factors. Unfortunately, control is usually more difficult in the social world than in the physical world; thus it is very difficult to successfully apply the scientific method to many questions about complex human behavior.

Precision in language is a third major component of the scientific method. Concepts are often confusing, obscure, and ambiguous. Scientific method tries to be precise and consistent in its use of language.

While there is much more to science than we can discuss here, we want you to keep in mind that scientific research, when conducted well, is one of our best sources of evidence because it emphasizes verifiability, control, and precision.

Problems with Research Findings

Unfortunately, the fact that research has been applied to a problem does not necessarily mean that the research evidence is dependable evidence or that the interpretations of the meaning of the evidence are accurate. Like appeals to any source, appeals to research evidence must be approached with caution. Also, some questions, particularly those that focus on human behavior, can be answered only tentatively even with the best of evidence. Thus, there are a number of important questions we want to ask about research studies before we decide how much to depend on their conclusions.

When communicators appeal to research as a source of evidence, you should remember the following:

1. Research varies greatly in *quality*; we should rely more on some research studies than others. There is well-done research and there is poorly done research, and we should rely more on the former. Because the research process is so complex and subject to so many external influences, even those well-trained in research practices sometimes conduct research studies that have important deficiencies; publication in a scientific journal does not guarantee that a research study is not flawed in important ways.

2. Research findings often contradict one another. Thus, *single* research studies presented out of the context of the family of research studies that - investigate the question often provide misleading conclusions. Research findings that most deserve our attention are those that have been repeated by more than one researcher or group of researchers. We need to always ask the question: "Have other researchers verified the findings?"

3. Research findings *do not prove* conclusions. At best, they *support* conclusions. Research findings do not speak for themselves! Researchers must always *interpret* the meaning of their findings, and all findings can be interpreted in more than one way. Thus, researchers' conclusions should not be treated as demonstrated "truths." When you encounter statements such as "research findings show . . ." you should retranslate them into "researchers interpret their research findings as showing . . ."

4. Like all of us, researchers have expectations, attitudes, values, and needs that bias the questions they ask, the way they conduct their research, and the way they interpret their research findings. For example, scientists often have an emotional investment in a particular hypothesis. When the American Sugar Institute is paying for your summer research grant, it is very difficult to then "find" that sugar consumption among teenagers is excessive. Like all fallible human beings, scientists may find it difficult to objectively treat data that conflict with their hypothesis. A major strength of scientific research is that it tries to make public its procedures and results so that others can judge the merit of the research and then try to replicate it. However, regardless of how objective a scientific report may seem, important subjective elements are always involved.

5. Speakers and writers often distort or simplify research conclusions. Major discrepancies may occur between the conclusion merited by the original research and the use of the evidence to support a communicator's beliefs. For example, researchers may carefully qualify their own conclusions in their original research report only to have the conclusions used by others without the qualifications.

6. Research "facts" change over time, especially claims about human behavior. For example, all of the following research "facts" have been reported by major scientific sources, yet have been "refuted" by recent research evidence:

Prozac is completely safe when taken by children.

It is important to drink eight glasses of water a day.

Depression is caused entirely by chemical imbalances in the brain.

Improper attachment to parents causes anti-social behavior in children.

7. Research varies in how artificial it is. Often, to achieve the goal of control, research loses some of its "real-world" quality. The more artificial the research, the more difficult it is to generalize from the research study to the world outside. The problem of research artificiality is especially evident in research studying complex social behavior. For example, social scientists will have people sit in a room with a computer to play "games" that involve testing people's reasoning processes. The researchers are trying to figure out why people make certain decisions when confronted with different scenarios. However, we should ask, "Is sitting at the computer while thinking through hypothetical situations too artificial to tell us much about the way people make decisions when confronted with real dilemmas?"

8. The need for financial gain, status, security, and other factors can affect research outcomes. Researchers are human beings, not computers. Thus, it is extremely difficult for them to be totally objective. For example, researchers who want to find a certain outcome through their research may interpret their results in such a way to find the desired outcome. Pressures to obtain grants, tenure, or other personal rewards might ultimately affect the way in which researchers interpret their data.

As you can see, despite the many positive qualities of research evidence, we need to avoid embracing research conclusions prematurely.

Clues for Evaluating Research Studies

Apply these questions to research findings to determine whether the findings are dependable evidence.

1. *What is the quality of the source of the report?* Usually, the most dependable reports are those published in peer-review journals, those in which a study is not accepted until it has been reviewed by a series of relevant experts. Usually—but not always—the more reputable the source, the better designed the study. So, try to find out all you can about the reputation of the source.

2. Other than the quality of the source, are there other clues included in the communication suggesting the research was well done? For example, *does the report detail any special strengths of the research?*

3. *Has the study been replicated?* Has more than one study reached the same conclusion? Findings, even when "statistically significant," can arise by chance alone. For example, when an association is repeatedly and consistently found in well-designed studies, like the link between smoking and cancer, then there is reason to believe it, at least until those who disagree can provide persuasive evidence for their point of view.

4. *How selective has the communicator been in choosing studies?* For example, have relevant studies with contradictory results been omitted? Has the researcher selected only those studies that support his point?

5. *Is there any evidence of strong-sense critical thinking?* Has the speaker or writer showed a critical attitude toward earlier research that was supportive of her point of view? Most conclusions from research need to be qualified because of research limitations. Has the communicator demonstrated a willingness to qualify?

6. *Is there any reason for someone to have distorted the research?* We need to be wary of situations in which the researchers *need* to find certain kinds of results.

7. *Are conditions in the research artificial and therefore distorted?* Always ask, "How similar are the conditions under which the research study was conducted to the situation the researcher is generalizing about?"

8. *How far can we generalize, given the research sample?* We discuss this question in depth in our next section.

9. *Are there any biases or distortions in the surveys, questionnaires, ratings, or other measurements that the researcher uses?* We need to have confidence that the researcher has measured accurately what she has wanted to measure. The problem of biased surveys and questionnaires is so pervasive in research that we discuss it in more detail in a later section.

Generalizing from the Research Sample

Speakers and writers usually use research reports to support generalizations, that is, claims about events in general. For example, "the medication was effective in treating cancer for the patients in the study" is not a generalization; "the medication cures cancer" is. The ability to generalize from research findings depends on the *number, breadth,* and *randomness* of events or people the researchers study.

The process of selecting events or persons to study is called *sampling.*

Because researchers can never study all events or people about which they want to generalize, they must choose some way to sample; and some ways are preferable to others. You need to keep several important considerations in mind when evaluating the research sample:

1. The sample must be large enough to justify the generalization or conclusion. In most cases, the more events or people researchers observe, the more dependable their conclusion. If we want to form a general belief about how often college students receive help from others on term papers, we are better off studying 100 college students than studying 10.

2. The sample must possess as much *breadth,* or diversity, as the types of events about which conclusions are to be drawn. For example, if researchers want to generalize about college students' drinking habits in general, their evidence should be based on the sampling of a variety of different kinds of college students in a variety of different kinds of college settings. Students at a small private school in the Midwest may have different drinking habits than students at a large public school on the West Coast; thus, a study of students attending only one school would lack breadth of sampling.

3. The more *random* the sample, the better. When researchers randomly sample, they try to make sure that all events about which they want to

generalize have an *equal chance* of getting sampled; they try to avoid a biased sample. Major polls, like the Gallop poll, for example, always try to sample randomly. This keeps them from getting groups of events or people that have biased characteristics. Do you see how each of the following samples has biased characteristics?

a. People who volunteer to be interviewed about frequency of sexual activity.

b. People who are at home at 2:30 P.M. to answer their phone.

c. Readers of a popular women's magazine who clip and complete mail-in surveys.

Thus, we want to ask of all research studies, "How many events or people did they sample, how much breadth did the sample have, and how random was the sample?"

A common problem that stems from not paying enough attention to the limits of sampling is for communicators to *overgeneralize* research findings. They state a generalization that is much broader than that warranted by the research. In Chapter 7, we referred to such overgeneralizing as the *Hasty Generalization* fallacy. Let's take a close look at a research overgeneralization:

> Alcohol consumption is at an all-time high at colleges nationwide. A recent survey conducted by Drinksville University found that of the 250 people surveyed, 89 percent drink on a semi-regular basis.

Sampling procedures prohibit such a broad generalization. The research report implies the conclusion can be applied to *all* campuses, when the research studied only one campus. We don't even know whether the conclusion can be applied to that campus, because we don't know how randomly researchers sampled from it. The research report is flawed because it greatly overgeneralizes.

Remember: We can generalize only to people and events that are like those that we have studied in the research!

Biased Surveys and Questionnaires

It's early evening. You have just finished dinner. The phone rings. "We're conducting a survey of public opinion. Will you answer a few questions?" If you answer "yes," you will be among thousands who annually take part in surveys— one of the research methods you will encounter most frequently. Think how often you hear the phrase "according to recent polls."

Surveys and questionnaires are usually used to measure people's attitudes and beliefs. Just how dependable are they? It depends! Survey responses are subject to many influences; thus, one has to be very cautious in interpreting their meaning. Let's examine some of these influences.

First, for survey responses to be meaningful, they must be answered honestly. That is, verbal reports need to mirror actual beliefs and attitudes. Yet, for a variety of reasons, people frequently shade the truth. For example, they may give answers they think they ought to give, rather than answers that reflect their true beliefs. They may experience hostility toward the questionnaire or toward the kind of question asked. They may give too little thought to the question. If you have ever been a survey participant, you can probably think of other influences.

Remember: You cannot assume that verbal reports accurately reflect true attitudes.

Second, many survey questions are ambiguous in their wording; the questions are subject to multiple interpretations. Different individuals may in essence be responding to different questions! For example, imagine the multiple possible interpretations of the following survey question: "Do you think there is quality programming on television?" The more ambiguous the wording of a survey, the less credibility you can place in the results.

You should always ask the question: "How were the survey questions worded?" Usually, the more specifically worded a question, the more likely that different individuals will interpret it similarly.

Third, surveys contain many *built-in biases* that make them even more suspect. Two of the most important are *biased wording* and *biased context.* Biased wording of a question is a common problem; a small change in how a question is asked can have a major effect on how a question is answered. Let's examine a conclusion based on a recent poll and then look at the survey question.

A college professor found that 86 percent of respondents believe that President Bush has failed the American people with respect to his handling of the war in Iraq.

Now let's look closely at the survey question: "What do you think about the President's misguided efforts in the war in Iraq?" Look carefully at this question. Do you see the built-in bias? The "leading" words are "the President's misguided efforts." Wouldn't the responses have been quite different if the question had read: "What do you think about the President's attempt to bring democracy, markets, and freedom to the Iraqi people?" Thus, the responses obtained here are not an accurate indicator of attitudes concerning President Bush's handling of the war in Iraq.

Survey and questionnaire data must always be examined for possible bias. *Look carefully at the wording of the questions!* Here is another example. We have emphasized the word that demonstrates the bias.

QUESTION: *Should poor people who* **refuse** *to get a job be allowed to receive welfare benefits?*

CONCLUSION: *Ninety-three percent of people responding believe poor people should not receive welfare benefits.*

The effect of *context* on an answer to a question can also be powerful. Even answers to identical questions can vary from poll to poll depending on how the questionnaire is presented and how the question is embedded in the survey. The following question was included in two recent surveys: "Do you think we should lower the drinking age from 21?" In one survey, the question was preceded by another question: "Do you think the right to vote should be given to children at the age of 18 as it currently is?" In the other survey, no preceding question occurred. Not surprisingly, the two surveys showed different results. Can you see how the context might have affected respondents?

Another important contextual factor is *length*. In long surveys, people may respond differently to later items than to earlier items simply because they get tired. *Be alert to contextual factors when evaluating survey results.*

Because the way people respond to surveys is affected by many unknown factors, such as the need to please or the interpretation of the question, should we ever treat survey evidence as good evidence? There are heated debates about this issue, but our answer is "yes," as long as we are careful and do not generalize further than warranted. Some surveys are more reputable than others. The better the quality of the survey, the more you should be influenced by the results.

Our recommendation is to examine survey *procedures* carefully before accepting survey *results*. Once you have ascertained the quality of the procedures, you can choose to generate your own *qualified generalization*—one that takes into account any biases you might have found. Even biased surveys can be informative; but you need to know the biases in order to not be unduly persuaded by the findings.

Critical Evaluation of a Research-Based Argument

Let's now use our questions about research to evaluate the following argument in which research evidence has been used to support a conclusion.

Parents who push their children to study frequently end up causing their children to dislike reading, a recent study argues. The researchers studied 56 children in the sixth grade and found that those who reported the greatest dislike for reading were the ones whose parents frequently forced them to read. Alternatively, students who reported enjoying reading had less domineering parents. "The more demanding the parents were with studying, the less likely the child was to enjoy reading on his or her own," claim Stanley and Livingstone in the August issue of *Educator's War Chest.* The study was conducted at Little Creek elementary school in Phoenix, Arizona. The study found that if not forced to study, children were more likely to pick up a book in their free time. "It seems that there is a natural inclination to rebel against one's parents in children, and one way to manifest this inclination is to refuse to read if the child's parents force the child to study," reported Stanley and Livingstone.

The research is presented here in an uncritical fashion. We see no sign of strong-sense critical thinking. The report makes no references to special strengths or weaknesses of the study, although it does provides some detail about the research procedures so that we can make judgments about its worth as the basis of a generalization. There is no indication of whether the study has been replicated. Also, we do not know how selective the communicator has been in choosing studies, nor how this research fits into the broader context of research on children and their enjoyment of reading. We do not know what benefits publishing this study may have had for the researchers.

Have the researchers and passage author overgeneralized? The sample is small—56—and it lacks breadth and randomness because it is restricted to one elementary school in the Southwest. We need to ask many questions about the sampling. How were these children selected? How was the study advertised to the parents? Could there have been a bias in the kind of parents willing to sign up for such a study? Would we have gotten similar results if we had randomly chosen families from a large number of schools throughout the country? This passage clearly illustrates a case of overgeneralization!

Are the questionnaires biased? Consider being a parent and completing a questionnaire about how controlling you are. Don't you think we could raise doubts about the accuracy of responses to such a questionnaire? Too little information is given about the wording of the questionnaires or about the arrangement of questionnaire items to judge the ambiguity of the item wording and the possibility of biased wording and biased context.

We have raised enough questions about the above passage to be wary of its factual claims. We would want to rely on much more research before we could conclude that these claims are dependable.

Let's now look at a very different source of evidence.

Case Examples as Evidence

> President of a large university: "Of course our students can move on to high paying jobs and further study at large universities. Why, just this past year we sent one of our students, Mary Nicexample, off to law school at Harvard. In her first year Mary remained in the top five percent of her class. Therefore, our students can certainly achieve remarkable success at elite universities."

A frequently used kind of evidence that contrasts markedly to the kind of research study that we have just described, which emphasized studying large representative samples, is the use of a detailed description of one or several individuals or events to support a conclusion. Such descriptions are usually based on observations or interviews and vary from being in depth and thorough to being superficial. We call such descriptions *case examples.*

Communicators often begin persuasive presentations with dramatic descriptions of cases. For example, one way to argue to increase the drinking age is to tell heart-wrenching stories of young people's dying in car accidents when the driver was young and drunk.

Case examples are often compelling to us because of their colorfulness and their interesting details, which make them easy to visualize. Political candidates have increasingly resorted to case examples in their speeches, knowing that the rich details of cases generate an emotional reaction. Such cases, however, should be viewed more as *striking examples or anecdotes* than as proof, and we must be very suspicious of their use as evidence.

Dramatic cases *appeal to our emotions* and distract us from seeking other more relevant research evidence. For example, imagine a story about a man who tortured and murdered his numerous victims. The human drama of these crimes may lead us to ignore the fact that such a case is rare and that over the past 30 years 119 inmates with capital sentences were found to be innocent and released from prison.

Be wary of striking case examples as proof!

Although case examples will be consistent with a conclusion, do not let that consistency fool you. Always ask yourself: "Is the example typical?" "Are there powerful counterexamples?" "Are there biases in how the example is reported?"

Are there times that case examples can be useful, even if they are not good evidence? Certainly! Like personal experiences, they demonstrate important *possibilities* and put a personal face on abstract statistics. They make it easier for people to relate to an issue and thus take more interest in it.

Analogies as Evidence

Look closely at the structure of the following brief arguments, paying special attention to the reason supporting the conclusion.

> Adults cannot learn all of the intricacies of new computer technology. Trying to teach adults new computer systems is like trying to teach an old dog new tricks.

> As an educator it is important to weed out problem students early and take care of the problems they present because one bad egg ruins the omelet.

These two arguments use *analogies* as evidence, a very different kind of evidence from what we have previously been evaluating. How do we decide whether it is good evidence? Before reading on, try to determine the persuasiveness of the two arguments.

Communicators often use *resemblance* as a form of evidence. They reason in the following way: "If these two things are alike in one respect, then they will probably be alike in other respects as well."

For example, when bipolar disorder (manic depression) was first identified, psychologists frequently treated it similarly to depression because both shared the common characteristics of severe depression. We reason in a similar fashion when we choose to buy a CD because a friend recommends it. We reason that because we resemble each other in a number of likes and dislikes, we will enjoy the same music.

An argument that uses a well-known similarity between two things as the basis for a conclusion about a relatively unknown characteristic of one of those things is an *argument by analogy*. Reasoning by analogy is a common way of presenting evidence to support a conclusion.

Analogies both stimulate insights and deceive us. For example, analogies have been highly productive in scientific and legal reasoning. When we infer conclusions about humans on the basis of research with mice, we reason by analogy. Much of our thinking about the structure of the atom is analogical reasoning. When we make a decision in a legal case, we may base that decision on the similarity of that case to preceding cases. For example, when judges approach the question of whether restricting pornographic material violates the constitutional protection of free speech and freedom of expression, they must decide whether the potentially obscene pornographic material is analogous to freedom of speech; thus, they reason by analogy. Such reasoning can be quite insightful and persuasive.

Identifying and Comprehending Analogies

Accurate analogies are powerful, but are often difficult for people to evaluate. Analogies compare two known things to allow the reader to better understand the relationship to something that is unfamiliar. To be able to identify such comparisons, it is important to understand how analogies are structured. The first part of an analogy involves a familiar object or concept. That object or concept is being compared to another familiar object or concept. The second part is the relationship between the familiar objects or concepts. This relationship is used to create a principle that can be used to assist the understanding of a different object or concept. Finally, the relationship of the new or unfamiliar object or concept is described in the same format as the known object or concept.

For example, "Relearning geometry is like riding a bike. Once you start, it all comes back to you." In the preceding analogy, riding a bicycle, the known, is used to explain relearning geometry, the unknown. We are familiar with the idea of getting on a bike after a period of time and "it all coming back to us" as we start to ride again. The analogy, therefore, explains relearning geometry in the same way, arguing if one simply starts to do geometry problems, remembering how to do such problems will simply come back to the person.

Once the nature and structure of analogies is understood, you should be able to identify analogies in arguments. It is especially important to identify analogies when they are used to set the tone of the conversation. Such analogies are used to "frame" an argument. To identify framing analogies, look for comparisons that are used to not only explain a point, but also to influence the direction a discussion will take.

For example, in the 2004 presidential election, the war in Iraq was an important issue. Opponents of the war used the analogy comparing the war in Iraq to the Vietnam War. The use of Vietnam as an analogy to the war in Iraq was not only an attempt to explain what is happening in Iraq now, but also to cause people to look negatively upon the war in Iraq. Conversely, proponents of the war in Iraq used the analogy comparing the war to World War II. World War II carries with it more positive connotations than does the Vietnam War, so this analogy was used to reframe the discussion in terms more favorable to the war in Iraq. Always look for comparisons that attempt to direct the reaction to an object through framing. A careful evaluation of framing analogies will prevent you from being misled by a potentially deceptive analogy.

Framing analogies is not the only thing to be wary of when looking for analogies in arguments. One must also be careful when evaluating arguments that use overly emotional comparisons. For example, one person in arguing against the estate tax recently compared the tax to the Holocaust. Who could possibly be in favor of a tax that is the equivalent of the Holocaust? However, we must evaluate the analogy to see whether it is really accurate or simply an emotion-laden comparison intended to coerce people into agreeing with a certain perspective by making the alternative seem ridiculous. After all, regardless of what one thinks about the estate tax, it is not responsible for the deaths of millions of people. Overly emotional analogies cloud the real issues in arguments and prevent substantive discourse. Try to identify comparisons made that contain significant emotional connotations to avoid being deceived by these analogies.

Evaluating Analogies

Because analogical reasoning is so common and has the potential to be both persuasive and faulty, you will find it very useful to recognize such reasoning and know how to systematically evaluate it. To evaluate the quality of an analogy, you need to focus on two factors.

1. The number of ways the two things being compared are similar and different.
2. The *relevance* of the similarities and the differences.

A word of caution: You can almost always find some similarities between any two things. So, analogical reasoning will not be persuasive simply because of many similarities. Strong analogies will be ones in which the two things we compare possess *relevant* similarities and lack *relevant* differences. All analogies try to illustrate underlying principles. *Relevant similarities and differences are ones that directly relate to the underlying principle illustrated by the analogy.*

Let's check out the soundness of the following argument by analogy.

> I do not allow my dog to run around the neighborhood getting into trouble, so why shouldn't I enforce an 8 o'clock curfew on my 16-year old? I am responsible for keeping my daughter safe, as well as responsible for what she might do when she is out. My dog stays in the yard, and I want my daughter to stay in the house. This way, I know exactly what both are doing.

A major similarity between a pet and a child is that both are thought of as not being full citizens with all the rights and responsibilities of adults. Plus, as the speaker asserts, he is responsible for keeping his dog and daughter safe. We note some relevant differences, however. A dog is a pet who lacks higher order thinking skills and cannot assess right and wrong. A daughter, however, is a human being with the cognitive capacity to tell when things are right and wrong and when she should not do something that might get her (or her parents) in trouble. Also, as a human, she has certain rights and deserves a certain amount of respect for her autonomy. Thus, because a daughter can do things a dog cannot, the differences are relevant in assessing the analogy. The failure of the analogy to allow for the above listed distinctions causes it to fail to provide strong support for the conclusion.

Another strategy that may help you evaluate reasoning by analogy is to *generate alternative analogies* for understanding the same phenomenon that the author or speaker is trying to understand. Such analogies may either support or contradict the conclusions inferred from the original analogy. If they contradict the conclusion, they then reveal problems in the initial reasoning by analogy.

For example, when authors argue that pornography should be banned because it is harmful to women, as well as to all who view it, they are using a particular analogy to draw certain conclusions about pornography: Pornography is like a form of discrimination, as well as a means by which people are taught women are nothing but sex objects. Others, however, have offered alternative analogies, arguing that pornography is "a statement of women's sexual liberation." Note how thinking about this different analogy may create doubts about the persuasiveness of the original analogy.

A productive way to generate your own analogies is the following:

1. Identify some important features of what you are studying.
2. Try to identify other situations with which you are familiar that have some similar features. Give free rein to your imagination. Brainstorm. Try to imagine diverse situations.
3. Try to determine whether the familiar situation can provide you with some insights about the unfamiliar situation.

For example, in thinking about pornography, you could try to think of other situations in which people repeatedly think something is demeaning because of the way people are treated in a given situation, or because of what watching something might cause others to do. Do segregation, racist/sexist jokes, or employment discrimination come to mind? How about arguments' claiming playing violent video games, watching action movies, or listening to heavy metal music causes children to act violently? Do they trigger other ways to think about pornography? You should now be capable of systematically evaluating the two brief analogical arguments at the beginning of this section. Ask the questions you need to ask to determine the structure of the argument.

Then, ask the questions to evaluate the argument. Look for relevant similarities and differences. Usually, the greater the ratio of relevant similarities to relevant differences, the stronger the analogy. An analogy is especially compelling if you can find *no* relevant difference and you can find good evidence that the relevant similarities do indeed exist.

We found a relevant difference that weakens each of our two initial sample analogies. Check your evaluation against our list.

> (First example) Learning computer skills involves cognitive capabilities well within those of your average adult; teaching "an old dog new tricks" involves training an animal with lower cognitive abilities, who is set in his ways, how to obey a command he may never have heard before. Learning computer skills is not the same as classically conditioning an animal.

> (Second example) The interactions of students in a classroom environment are very complex. The effect any one student might have on the group cannot easily be determined, just as the effects the group might have on the individual are difficult to predict. Conversely, a rotten egg will definitely spoil any food made from it. Also, it is problematic to think of people as unchanging objects, such as rotten eggs, that have no potential for growth and change.

Analogies that trick or deceive us fit our definition of a reasoning fallacy; such deception is called the Faulty Analogy fallacy.

F: **Faulty Analogy:**   Occurs when an analogy is proposed in which there are important relevant dissimilarities.

In one sense, all analogies are faulty, because they make the mistaken assumption that because two things are alike in one or more respects, they are necessarily alike in some other important respect. It is probably best for you to think of analogies as varying from very weak to very strong. But even the best analogies are only suggestive. Thus if an author draws a conclusion about one case from a comparison to another case, then she should provide further evidence to support the principle revealed by the most significant similarity.

Summary

This chapter has continued our focus on the evaluation of evidence. We have discussed the following kinds of evidence: observation, research studies, case examples, and analogies. Each source has its strengths and weaknesses. Usually, you can rely most on those claims that writers or speakers support directly by extensive scientific research. However, many issues have not been settled by scientific research, and consequently, communicators must rely on research that is not conclusive and on other sources of evidence. You should be especially wary of claims supported by biased observation, dramatic case examples, poorly designed research, or faulty analogies. When you encounter *any* evidence, you should try to determine its quality by asking, *"How good is the evidence?"*

Practice Exercises

(?) *Critical Question:* **How good is the evidence?**

Evaluate each of these practice passages by examining the quality of the evidence provided.

Passage 1

Are children of alcoholics more likely to be alcoholics themselves? In answering the question, researchers sampled 451 people in Alcoholics Anonymous to see how many would say that one, or both, of their parents were alcoholics. People in AA used in the study currently attend AA somewhere in Ohio, Michigan, or Indiana and were asked by people in charge of the local AA programs to volunteer to fill out a survey. The research found that 77 percent of the respondents had at least one parent they classified as an alcoholic. The study also surveyed 451 people randomly from the same states who claim not to be heavy drinkers. Of the non-heavy drinkers, 23 percent would label at least one of their parents as alcoholic.

Passage 2

I think California's "three strikes law" is a great idea. Why should criminals be given unlimited chances to continue to re-offend? We give a batter only three attempts to swing and hit a ball, so why does a criminal deserve any better? Three swings and misses and you are out; three offenses and convictions and you are in, jail that is.

Passage 3

One of the greatest symbols of the U.S. is the American flag. While cases in the past have defended desecration of the flag as symbolic speech I argue, "Where is the speech in such acts?" I do not believe allowing people to tarnish the flag and thus attack everything that America stands for is the same as allowing free speech. If you have something bad to say about the U.S., say it, but do not cheapen the flag with your actions. Many Americans died to keep that flag flying.

Those who want to support flag burning and other such despicable acts are outnumbered. Last month, 75 people were surveyed in a restaurant in Dallas, Texas, and were asked if they supported the unpatriotic desecration of the American flag in an attempt to express some sort of anti-American idea. Ninety-three percent responded that they were not in favor of desecration of the American flag. Therefore, our national lawmakers should pass a law protecting the American flag against such horrible actions.

Sample Responses

Passage 1

CONCLUSION: *Children of alcoholics are more likely to become alcoholics than are children of non-alcoholics.*

REASON: *More alcoholics than non-alcoholics reported a substantially higher rate of having an alcoholic parent.*

Note that the results presented are from one study without reference to how typical these results are. We also do not know where this information was published, so we can make no assessments regarding how rigorously the study was reviewed before publication. However, we can ask some useful questions about the study. The sample size is quite large, but its breadth is questionable. Although multiple states were sampled, to what extent are the people in the AA programs in these states typical of alcoholics across the nation? Also, how do alcoholics in AA compare to alcoholics who have not sought help? Perhaps the most important sampling problem was the lack of a random sample. While the self-reported non-alcoholics were randomly selected in the three states, the respondents in AA were selected on a voluntary basis. Do those who volunteered to talk about their parents differ greatly from those who did not volunteer? If there is a difference between the volunteers and non-volunteers, then the sample is biased.

How accurate are the rating measurements? First, no definition for alcoholic for those answering the survey is given beyond currently being in AA. In addition, we are not told of any criteria given to the research participants for rating parents as alcoholic. Thus we are uncertain of the accuracy of the judgments about whether someone was an alcoholic. Also, problematic is the fact that the selection of the supposed control group of non-alcoholics is based on self-assessment. We know that there is a socially acceptable answer of not being an alcoholic, and people tend to give socially acceptable answers when they are known. This response tendency could also bias the sampling in the supposed control group. We would want to know more about the accuracy of these ratings before we could have much confidence in the conclusion.

Passage 2

CONCLUSION: *Three strikes law for criminal offenses are desirable.*

REASON: *Allowing a criminal to offend three times is like allowing a batter in baseball to swing and miss three times.*

The author is arguing the desirability of the three strikes law by drawing an obvious analogy to baseball. The similarity the author is focusing on is that three chances for a batter to hit a ball is much like the three chances awarded to convicted offenders to shape up or to be put in jail for a long time. But simply saying three criminal offenses deserves harsh punishment ignores the complexity involved in criminal sentencing. For example, while a swing and a miss is a strike regardless of the type of pitch the pitcher throws, we might feel context is very important for sentencing criminals. What if the third offense is something very minor? Does it make sense to punish the criminal severely for a third offense regardless of what the other two were? Because of an important relevant difference, we conclude that this analogy is not very relevant.

CRITICAL QUESTION SUMMARY: WHY THIS QUESTION IS IMPORTANT

How Good Is the Evidence?

When an author offers a reason in support of a conclusion, you want to know *why* you should believe that reason. By identifying the evidence offered in support of a reason, you are taking another step in evaluating the worth of the reason. If the evidence that supports the reason is good, the reason better supports the conclusion. Thus, you might be more willing to accept the author's conclusion if the author offers good evidence in support of a reason, which in turn provides good support for the conclusion.

CHAPTER

10

ARE THERE RIVAL CAUSES?

We begin this chapter with a story.

> An inquisitive little boy noticed that the sun would show up in the sky in the morning and disappear at night. Puzzled by where the sun went, the boy tried to watch the sunset really closely. However, he still could not figure out where the sun was going. Then, the boy also noticed that his babysitter showed up in the mornings and left at night. One day he asked his babysitter where she went at night. The babysitter responded, "I go home." Linking his babysitter's arrival and departure with the coming of day and night, he concluded that his babysitter's leaving, caused the sun to also go home.

This story clearly illustrates a common difficulty in the use of evidence: trying to figure out what caused something to happen. We cannot determine an intelligent approach to avoiding a problem or encouraging a particular positive outcome until we understand the causal pattern that gave rise to the phenomenon in the first place. For example, we want to know what caused the steady rise in oil prices in the United States over the last few years. Or, *why* the suicide rate among professionals increased over the last 10 years?

The story also shows a very common difficulty in using evidence to prove that something caused something else—the problem of *rival causes*. The fictional little boy offered one interpretation of his observations: the sun sets at night because my babysitter goes home. We expect that you can see another very plausible explanation for why the sun sets.

Although rival causes will rarely be as obvious as they are in our story, you will frequently encounter experts presenting one hypothesis to explain events or research findings when other plausible hypotheses could also explain them. Usually, these experts will not reveal rival causes to you because they do not want to detract from the sound of certainty associated with their claims; you will have to produce them. Doing so can be especially helpful as you decide "how good is the evidence?" The existence of multiple, plausible rival causes for events reduces our confidence in the cause originally offered by the author.

Searching for rival causes will always be appropriate when a speaker or writer presents you with some evidence and offers a cause to explain it.

Critical Question: **Are there rival causes?**

Attention: A rival cause is a plausible alternative explanation that can explain why a certain outcome occurred.

When to Look for Rival Causes

You need to look for rival causes when you have good reason to believe that the writer or speaker is using evidence to support a claim about the cause of something. The word *cause* means "to bring about, make happen, or affect." Communicators can indicate causal thinking to you in a number of ways. We have listed a few.

X has the effect of . . .	X deters . . .
X leads to . . .	X increases the likelihood . . .
X influences . . .	X determines . . .
X is a factor in . . .	X contributes to . . .
X is linked to . . .	X is associated with . . .

These clues to causal thinking should help you recognize when a communicator is making a causal claim. Once you note such a claim, be alert to the possibility of rival causes.

The Pervasiveness of Rival Causes

On the afternoon of March 28, 1941, Virginia Woolf wrote two letters, sealed them, and placed them on the mantle. She quickly put on her coat, grabbed her walking stick, and headed outside. She crossed the meadows to the river Ouse, where she put large stones into her coat pocket and threw herself into the river, committing suicide.

Authors have offered numerous hypotheses to explain this event, including the following:

> 1. Virginia Woolf had a fear of impending madness. She had a history of mental illness and depression. Also, given the recent outbreak of World War II and her history of an inability to deal with aggression, Virginia decided it would be best if she took her own life.[1]

> 2. Some psychologists argue Virginia Woolf had an intense attachment with her father. The attachment was so strong that Virginia developed to be much like her father in many significant ways. One important event in Virginia's life, therefore, was watching her father's deteriorating health when Virginia was in her early twenties. She never forgot about her father's suffering and deterioration. So, when Virginia was 59 years old and feeling that her writing was beginning to deteriorate, she took her life in order to avoid identifying with, and in essence becoming, her dying father.[2]

> 3. Virginia Woolf was disillusioned with her marriage to Leonard Woolf. The two had a sexless marriage, and Virginia found companionship in an extra-marital lesbian relationship. Virginia's homosexuality put tremendous strain on the marriage that was in turn only made worse by the fact that Leonard probably had several affairs. Virginia was a very jealous person and did not take lightly to these affairs. Her dissatisfaction with the condition of her marriage led her to take her life.[3]

Woolf's own writing leads to any number of possible causes for her suicide.

Now, let's leave Virginia Woolf's suicide for a moment and examine a different event in need of explanation—the findings of a research study.

> A researcher reported that eating celery helps curb aggression. 151 women were surveyed, and 95 percent who reported eating celery on a regular basis also reported low levels of aggression, or overall irritability. Of the portion of women who do not eat celery on a regular basis, 53 percent reported frequent feelings of irritability, agitation, and aggression.

[1]Alma Halbert Bond, *Who Killed Virginia Woolf: A Psychobiography* (New York: Human Sciences Press, 1989): 15–19.

[2]Ibid., pp. 59–63.

[3]Ibid., pp. 62–63.

In this study, the researcher probably began with the hypothesis that eating celery *causes* reduction of aggressive impulses, and he found evidence consistent with that hypothesis. But let us offer several rival, or different, causes for the same findings.

1. Research participants were highly suggestible, and the *expectation of low levels of aggression* was responsible for the reported differences; like the sugar pill placebo effect in medicine, believing that eating celery lowers aggression might have stimulated a number of physical and mental processes that caused participants to feel less aggression.

2. Participants wanted to please the researchers; thus, they reported feeling low levels of aggression, even though they did experience some aggressive feelings.

3. Nothing is known about the women involved in the study. It is entirely plausible that those who eat celery are health conscious, and thus are more likely to exercise. The increased amounts of exercise can be an outlet for aggression, and thus lower feelings of aggression. Those who do not eat celery regularly may not exercise as often and thus do not have an outlet for their aggression.

Now, let's leave the research laboratory for a moment and move to the national pages of our newspapers and examine an argument related to crime statistics.

Since 1993, the levels of serious violent crime in the United States have decreased steadily. It is obvious that the heavy focus we place on law enforcement is no longer necessary. People are becoming civic minded and are choosing to no longer pursue a life of crime. Money spent on law enforcement can now better be spent elsewhere.

The hypothesis offered by the writer is that people's increasing civic engagement is the cause of the decrease in violent crimes over the last 12 years. But, let's again generate some plausible rival causes:

1. Violent crime rates have decreased because of the increased focus on law enforcement the writer is specifically calling to be cut. An increased concern with law enforcement, and not the civic concerns of citizens, caused violent crime levels to decrease.

2. Recent legislative actions have increased the punishments associated with violent crimes. These increased punishments make the costs of committing a violent crime far outweigh the benefits of committing violent crimes. People are not more civic minded, rather they are looking out for their own personal interests.

3. The booming economy in the 1990s could have decreased the number of people in poverty. Given that the poor are typically the perpetrators of what we call violent crimes, fewer poor people would lower the violent crime rate.

Now, let's examine some important lessons that can be learned from Virginia Woolf's suicide, the celery research study, and the crime statistics.

Lessons Learned

1. Many kinds of events are open to explanation by rival causes.
2. Experts can examine the same evidence and "discover" different causes to explain it.
3. Most communicators will provide you with only their favored causes; the critical reader or listener must generate rival causes.
4. Generating rival causes is a creative process; usually such causes will not be obvious.
5. Finally, the certainty of a particular causal claim is inversely related to the number of plausible rival causes. Hence, identifying the multiple rival causes gives the critical thinker the proper sense of intellectual humility.

In the following sections, we explore the implications of these lessons for the critical thinker.

Detecting Rival Causes

Locating rival causes is much like being a good detective. When you recognize situations in which rival causes are possible, you want to ask yourself questions like:

? Can I think of any other way to interpret the evidence?

? What else might have caused this act or these findings?

? If I looked at this from another point of view, what might I see as important causes?

? If this interpretation is incorrect, what other interpretation might make sense?

The Cause or *A* Cause

The youth are exhibiting an alarming increase in the rate of depression among elementary aged children. Talk show hosts begin to interview the experts about *the* cause. It is genetic. It is the prevalence of teasing among peer groups. It is parental neglect. It is too much TV news coverage of terrorism and wars. It is lack of religion. It is stress. The experts may *claim* to have the answer, but they are not likely to *know* it. That is because a frequently made error is to look for a simple, single cause of an event when it is really the result of a combination of many *contributory* causes—a cause that helps to create a total set of conditions necessary for the event to occur.

Multiple contributory causes occur more often than do single causes in situations involving the characteristics or activities of humans. In many cases, the best causal explanation is one that combines a considerable number of causes that *only together* are sufficient to bring about the event. So, the best answer experts can give to the talk show hosts' question is "We don't know *the* cause for such events, but we can speculate about possible causes that might have contributed to the event." Thus, when we are searching for rival causes, we need to remember that any single cause that we identify is much more likely to be a contributory cause than *the* cause.

When communicators fail to consider the complexity of causes, they commit the following reasoning fallacy:

F: **Causal Oversimplification:** Explaining an event by relying on causal factors that are insufficient to account for the event or by overemphasizing the role of one or more of these factors.

In some sense, almost all causal explanations are oversimplifications; thus you want to be fair to communicators who offer explanations that do not include *every* possible cause of an event. Causal conclusions, however, should include sufficient causal factors to convince you that they are not too greatly oversimplified, or the author should make clear to you that the causal factor she emphasizes in her conclusion is only one of a number of possible contributing causes—**a** cause, not **the** cause.

Rival Causes and Scientific Research

Scientific research attempts to isolate some of the most important contributing causes from other extraneous causes and provides a major source of hypotheses about what causes events in our world. Researchers start with tentative beliefs—hypotheses—about causes of events. For example, when a massive wave killed thousands of people, researchers generated many hypotheses about the cause of tsunamis. One hypothesis was that tsunamis are caused by massive underwater earthquakes.

Once a hypothesis has been firmly established by dependable research evidence, it changes from a hypothesis to a law. In the domain of complex human behavior, however, there are very few established general laws. Stated claims like "fundamentalism causes terrorism," and "tax cuts cause economic growth" sound like laws, but we need to remain skeptical of the generalizability of such claims. They must currently be viewed as hypotheses, not laws, and are best stated as follows: "fundamentalism may be a contributing cause in the decision to resort to terrorism," and "tax cuts may be a contributing cause in stimulating economic growth."

Then, what should you do when speakers or writers use findings from research studies to conclude that one event causes another? First, remember that their conclusion should be viewed as **a** cause, not **the** cause. Then try to find out as much as you can about the research procedures used to produce the findings that support the hypothesis. Finally, try to determine rival causes that might explain the findings. The more plausible rival causes that can account for the findings, the less faith you should have in the hypothesis favored by the communicator.

Let's use the following argument to practice detecting rival causes.

Playing violent video games for long periods of time appears to increase the likelihood that a child will physically assault another child. The results confirm the general suspicion that violent video games cause violence in children. The relevant research findings are from the Center for Preventing Youth Violence, which enrolled 1,001 male children from across the United States. One-third of the children played "violent" video games, one-third played "non-violent" video games, and the remaining third did not play any video games. The children played several hours of video games alone every day for two weeks. At the end of the two weeks, the children from the different groups were put into a room with toys so that they could play together. Those children who played violent video games were more likely to get into physical altercations with other children than were those who played "non-violent" video games, or no video games at all.

Should parents take away all of their children's "violent" video games? Not until they consider rival causes! How else might one explain these group differences?

First, let's outline the reasoning:

> CONCLUSION: (Researchers' hypothesis) *Playing violent video games appears to cause an increase in violence among children.*

> REASON: (Researchers' evidence) *Research study showed children who played violent video games were more likely to get into physical altercations with other children than were those children who did not play violent video games.*

Note that the words *appears to cause* in the conclusion tell us the researchers are making a causal claim about the evidence. But other hypotheses can explain this evidence.

The report fails to tell us how the children were selected into the three different groups. It is possible that the children were allowed to self-select what games they play, and perhaps children who are more likely to be violent tend to choose "violent" video games. If so, it is possible the researcher has the causal link reversed. Also, nothing is revealed as to how the "play" situation was set up for the children. Perhaps the room or selection of toys was set up in such a way to encourage physical altercations among those who played the "violent" video games. We bet you can think of other reasons these groups—violent video game players and not—differ in their likelihood of resorting to physical violence.

We cannot make you aware of all possible rival causes. In the following selections, however, we provide several clues for finding common rival causes.

Rival Causes for Differences Between Groups

One of the most common ways for researchers to try to find a cause for some event is to *compare groups*. For example, you will frequently encounter the following kinds of references to group comparisons:

Researchers compared an experimental group to a control group.

One group received treatment X; the other group didn't.

A group with learning disabilities and a group without learning disabilities.

When researchers find differences between groups, they often conclude, "Those differences support our hypothesis." For example, a researcher might compare a group of people trying to lose weight treated with a new drug with a control group of people trying to lose weight that does not get the new drug, find that the groups differ in their weight loss, and then conclude that the drug caused the difference. The problem is that *research groups almost always differ in more than one important way,* and thus group differences often are consistent with multiple causes. Thus, when you see communicators use findings of differences between groups to support one cause, always ask, "Are there rival causes that might also explain the differences in the groups?"

Let's take a look at a study that compares groups and try to detect rival causes.

> In a recent research study, students who prepare for a standardized test by taking a special course designed to teach students how to take the test have scored higher than students who prepare for the same standardized test by reviewing several books about the test.

Here we have two groups: the students who take the class and the students who read a few books. The question we need to ask is, "Did these two groups differ in important ways other than the test preparation they experienced?" Did you think of either of the following possible important differences between the two groups that might account for test score differences?

- *Differences in students' academic (and economic) background.* It is possible that the course costs a substantial sum of money, and only those students who had the money could afford to take the class. Moreover, it is also possible that those students who could afford the money for the class also could afford better private school education before taking the test, and thus start off from a privileged position in comparison with the students who did not take the class.

- *Differences in motivation.* Perhaps the students who signed up for the class are the students who really want to excel in the test. Students who read a few books might be less interested in scoring really well on the standardized test. Alternatively, the students might have chosen study methods based on how they best learn. It is possible that those who learn best in a class setting might be predisposed to do well on standardized tests.

You probably came up with other important differences. Remember: *Many factors can cause research groups to differ!*

Confusing Causation with Association

We have an inherent tendency to "see" events that are associated, or that "go together," as events that cause one another. That is, we conclude that because characteristic X (e.g., amount of energy bars consumed) is associated with characteristic Y (e.g., performance in an athletic event), that X therefore causes Y. The following are examples of such reasoning:

1. Classes with larger numbers of students enrolled tend to experience high rates of students' skipping class.
2. More red cars than any other color are pulled over for speeding; therefore, the color of the car affects how fast it goes.

When we think this way, we are, however, often very wrong! Why? Usually multiple hypotheses can explain why X and Y "go together." In fact, there are at least four different kinds of hypotheses to account for any such relationship. Knowing what these are will help you discover rival causes. Let's illustrate each of the four with a research example.

> A recent study reported that "smoking combats the flu." The researchers studied 525 smokers and found that 67 percent of the smokers did not have the flu once over the last three years. The researchers hypothesized that the nicotine in the smoke from cigarettes destroys the flu virus before it can spread and cause sickness.

Should people who are feeling under the weather run out and start smoking to prevent the onset of the flu? Not yet. Before they do, they should contemplate each of four potential explanations for the research findings.

Explanation 1: *X is a cause of Y.* (Smoking does indeed kill the flu virus.)

Explanation 2: *Y is a cause of X.* (Feeling healthy, or feeling the beginning of what might be the flu, causes people to smoke.)

Explanation 3: *X and Y are associated because of some third factor, Z.* (Smoking and being without the flu are both caused by related factors, such as frequent washing of the hands after smoking prevents the spread of the flu virus.)

Explanation 4: *X and Y influence each other.* (People who do not usually catch the flu have a tendency to smoke, and the smoke may affect some potential illnesses.)

Remember: *Association or correlation does not prove causation!*

Yet much evidence to prove causation is only based on association or correlation. When an author supports a hypothesis by pointing to an association between characteristics, always ask, "Are there other causes that explain the association?"

Test yourself on the following:

A recent study reported that "ice cream causes crime." The researchers studied ice cream sales and crime rates over the last five years in the ten largest U.S. cities and found that as ice cream sales increase, so does the crime rate. The researchers hypothesized that the consumption of ice cream triggers a chemical reaction in one's brain causing the individual to have an inclination toward crime.

We hope you can now see that people who eat ice cream need not be concerned that they are about to commit a crime. What rival causes did you think of? Couldn't the increased summer heat account for the association between ice cream sales (X) and crime (Y)?

This confusion between correlation and causation is as understandable as it is dangerous. A cause will indeed precede its effect. But many things preceded that effect. Most of them were not causal.

You should now be able to identify two common causal reasoning fallacies by attending to the above four possible explanations of why events might be associated:

F: **Confusion of Cause and Effect:**   Confusing the cause with the effect of an event or failing to recognize that the two events may be influencing each other.

F: **Neglect of a Common Cause:**   Failure to recognize that two events may be related because of the effects of a common third factor.

Confusing "After this" with "Because of this"

Shortly after the 2004 Summer Olympics where Michael Phelps won six gold medals and two bronze medals, the price of college tuition nationwide once again increased. Does this mean we can attribute the price of college tuition to Michael Phelps' Olympic success? No. There are many other possible causes. If we were to infer such a conclusion, we would be illustrating a very common way that people confuse causation with association.

Often, we try to explain a particular event as follows: Because event B *followed* event A, then event A *caused* event B. Such reasoning occurs because human beings have a strong tendency to believe that if two events occur close together in time, the first one must have caused the second one.

To appreciate the flaw in this reasoning, pick up today's newspaper and make a list of what is going on in the world. Then pick up yesterday's newspaper and make a similar list. Could you conclude that the events of yesterday are causing the events of today? Clearly not. For example, yesterday's news contained more stories about the war in Iraq, and today's news reported that IBM is attempting to buy a start up firm to advance open-source software. It is highly unlikely that events in Iraq caused IBM's attempt to expand its business. Many events that occur after other events in time are not caused by the preceding events. When we wrongly conclude that the first event causes the second because it preceded it, we commit the *Post hoc, ergo propter hoc* (meaning: "after this, therefore because of this") fallacy, or, for short, the Post hoc fallacy. Such reasoning is responsible for many superstitious beliefs. For example, you may have written an excellent paper while wearing a particular hat, so now you always insist on wearing the same hat when you write papers.

F: **Post hoc Fallacy:**   Assuming that a particular event, B, is caused by another event, A, simply because B follows A in time.

The following examples further illustrate the problem with this kind of reasoning.

> "The quarter I found yesterday must be lucky. Since I have found it I got an A on a really hard test, my least favorite class was canceled, and my favorite movie was on TV last night." (Never mind the fact that I studied really hard for my test, my professor has a six-year old who recently had the flu, and the TV schedule is made far in advance of my finding a quarter.)

> "Ever since September 11th, 2001, large numbers of people have been afraid to fly, and airlines are suffering financially because of it." (But perhaps it is also relevant that the economy was suffering before, and continued to suffer after September 11, and the weak economy could mean that people have less disposable income with which to purchase airplane tickets.)

As you might guess, political and business leaders are fond of using the Post hoc argument, especially when it works in their favor. For example, they tend to take credit for anything good that takes place after they assumed their leadership role and to place blame elsewhere for anything bad that happens.

Remember: The finding that one event follows another in time does not by itself prove causation; it may be only a coincidence. When you see such reasoning, always ask yourself, "Are there rival causes that could account for the event?" and, "Is there any good evidence other than the fact that one event followed the other event in time?"

Explaining Individual Events or Acts

Why did Mount St. Helen's erupt again in 2004? What caused the increase in alcohol prices? Why did Martha Stuart engage in insider trading?

Like our question about Virginia Woolf's suicide, these questions seek explanations of individual historical events. Scientific research studies cannot answer the questions. Instead, we must search the past for clues. Such a search makes us highly susceptible to reasoning errors for several reasons. A few of these are especially important to remember.

First, as we saw in Virginia Woolf's case, so many different stories for the same event can "make sense." Second, the way we explain events is greatly influenced by social and political forces, as well as by individual psychological forces. For example, men view the cause of drug abuse differently than women, and Democrats might view the causes of poverty differently from Republicans.

Also, a common bias is "the *fundamental attribution error*," in which we typically overestimate the importance of personal tendencies relative to situational factors in interpreting the behavior of others. That is, we tend to see the cause of other's behavior as coming from within (their personal characteristics) rather than from without (situational forces.) So, for example, when someone steals something from someone else, we are likely to view the stealing initially as a result of a tendency of the person to be immoral or to be inconsiderate. However, we should also consider the role of outside circumstances, such as poverty or an honest mistake.

Another kind of common psychological error is to start with a limited number of possible causes and then to interpret additional information (even if it is irrelevant) as corroborating these existing hypotheses, rather than keeping the information separate or generating new, perhaps more complex, hypotheses. Our tendency is to simplify the world; yet often explanations require much complexity. Explaining events is not as simple as frequently portrayed by guest experts on the popular talk shows.

How can we know whether we have a "good" explanation of a particular event or set of events? We can never know for sure. But we can make some progress by asking critical questions.

Be wary of accepting the first interpretation of an event you encounter. Search for rival causes and try to compare their credibility. We must accept the fact that *many* events do not have a simple explanation.

Evaluating Rival Causes

The more plausible the rival causes that you come up with, the less faith you can have in the initial explanation offered, at least until further evidence has been considered. As a critical thinker, you will want to assess as best you can how each of the alternative explanations fits the available evidence, trying to be sensitive to your personal biases.

In comparing causes, we suggest that you apply the following criteria:

1. their logical soundness;
2. their consistency with other knowledge that you have; and
3. their previous success in explaining or predicting events.

USING THIS CRITICAL QUESTION

Every assertion about causation should trigger immediate curiosity in the mind of a critical thinker. But are there alternative causes for the phenomenon? Asking someone to consider rival causes is constructive criticism at its finest. Your objective in doing so is to find a better causal explanation.

Evidence and Your Own Writing and Speaking

The last three chapters have indirectly provided you with a clue for effective communication. Your audience will be justifiably impressed when you provide strong and sufficient evidence for your claims. But implicit in this clue is a warning: Your audience expects and should demand that your claims are supported by thorough evidence. Satisfying this demand is one of your greatest challenges as a writer and speaker.

Summary

Factual claims about the causes of events are weakened when other claims about the causes can be offered. Such claims are *rival causes*.

A common logical error in explaining observations is to confuse causation with association. Thus, always ask what other causes might explain observed associations. Be especially alert to the Post hoc fallacy.

(?) *Critical Question: **Are there rival causes?***

Practice Exercises

Each of the following examples provides an argument to support a causal claim. Try to generate rival causes for such claims. Then try to determine how much you have weakened the author's claim by knowledge of rival causes.

Passage 1

Oranges to combat the blues. Researchers have recently revealed that eating two oranges a day can help alleviate depression. Researchers studied 13 patients who had feelings of depression. After three weeks of eating two oranges a day, 9 of the 13 people reported improvement in their condition. The researchers hypothesize that the citric acid and vitamin C in oranges helps to stimulate serotonin production, helping to combat depression.

Passage 2

Why did the corporate executive steal funds from his business? A close look at his life can provide a clear and convincing answer. The executive comes from a very successful family where his parents are doctors and his siblings are lawyers. As a corporate executive, he was not making as much money as his family members. Also, the executive believes heavily in the American dream and the idea that if one works hard enough that person will succeed. However, despite his hard work the executive has had a number of recent business failures, including losing a substantial sum of money in the stock market. To make matters worse, his children need braces. To live up to expectations, become a success, and provide for his family, the executive had to steal the money from his business.

Passage 3

According to a recent study, one of the major causes of violence in schools is listening to aggressive heavy metal music. Researches studied more than 100 cases of "serious" violence within schools, and have found that 68% of the children involved in the violence listened to heavy metal music. These children would frequently come to school with headphones, listening to this music, as well as wearing clothing from heavy metal bands. Frequently these heavy metal songs discuss violence, and therefore are a direct cause of school violence.

Sample Responses ───────────────────────────────────

Passage 1

CONCLUSION: *Eating oranges helps alleviate depression.*

REASON: *9 of 13 patients who ate oranges experienced improvement with their depression.*

Can anything else account for the change besides eating oranges? Yes; the researcher fails to rule out many obvious alternative explanations. For example, the patients might have *expected* to get better, and these *expectancies* might have led to feeling better. Also, they knew the purpose of eating oranges, and a rival cause is that they *tried to please* the researchers by reporting that they felt better. We can also hypothesize that external events during the three-week treatment period caused the change. Perhaps during the three weeks of treatment, for example, the weather was especially good, and these people spent much more time exercising outside than usual, which could also help alleviate depression. Another possibility is that these people were suffering from a form of depression from which they could naturally expect to recover in a short period of time. Can you locate other rival causes?

Passage 2

CONCLUSION: *The executive stole money from his company to compete with his family members, to show that he is not a failure, and to provide for his family.*

REASON: *The executive was probably concerned with all of the above elements.*

It is possible that all of the above factors were important in causing the corporate executive to steal from his company. But many other people in society have the same pressures put upon them and they do not resort to illegal means to obtain money. Are there other possible causes for such behavior? As in the case of Virginia Woolf, we suspect there may be many other plausible explanations. Before we could conclude that these stresses in the executive's life are the causal factors, we would want to know more about his childhood and more about recent events in his life. For example, has the corporate executive had any recent disagreements with his boss? Had he been using drugs? Had he had any recent highly stressful experiences? Did he have a history of stealing? After the fact, we can always find childhood experiences that make sense as causes of adult behavior. Before we draw causal conclusions, however, we must seek more evidence to prove that the one set of events caused the other than the mere fact that one set of events preceded the other set. We must also be wary not to fall victims to the fundamental attribution error and be certain to consider external causal factors, as well as internal ones.

CRITICAL QUESTION SUMMARY: WHY THIS QUESTION IS IMPORTANT

Are There Rival Causes?

While an author might offer an explanation for why certain events occurred, other explanations might be plausible. When you try to identify rival causes, you are finding alternative explanations for an event. If you can identify alternative explanations, you must decide whether you should believe the author's explanation or one of the other explanations. If the author does not provide reasons for why you should accept her explanation over other explanations, you should not be willing to accept her explanation and, ultimately, her conclusion. Thus, looking for rival causes is another step in deciding whether to accept or reject an argument.

CHAPTER 11

ARE THE STATISTICS DECEPTIVE?

How much should you be persuaded by the following passage?

> The adjective "Kafkaesque," exists in more than 250 different languages, suggesting that his work has had a major impact all over the world.

You should not be very impressed by the above reasoning. The argument *deceives us with statistics*!

One of the most frequent kinds of evidence that authors present is "statistics." You have probably often heard people use the following phrase to help support their argument: "I have statistics to prove it." We use statistics (often inappropriately) to rate the performance of a new movie, to measure the sales of a new product, to judge the moneymaking capabilities of certain stocks, to determine the likelihood of the next card's being the ace, to measure graduation rates for different colleges, to measure alcohol content in a given beverage, to record frequency of different groups' having sex, and to provide input for many other issues.

Statistics are evidence expressed as numbers. Such evidence can seem quite impressive because numbers make evidence appear to be very scientific and precise, as though it represents "the facts." Statistics, however, can, and often do, lie! They do not necessarily prove what they appear to prove.

As a critical thinker, you should strive to detect erroneous statistical reasoning. In a few short paragraphs, we cannot show you all the different ways

155

that people can "lie with statistics." However, this chapter will provide some general strategies that you can use to detect such deception. In addition, it will alert you to flaws in statistical reasoning by illustrating a number of the most common ways that authors misuse statistical evidence.

(?) *Critical Question:* **Are the statistics deceptive?**

Unknowable and Biased Statistics

The first strategy for locating deceptive statistics is to try to find out as much as you can about how the statistics were obtained. Can we know precisely the number of people in the United States who cheat on their taxes, have premarital sex, drink and drive, run red lights, use illegal drugs, hit a car in a parking lot and left without informing anyone, buy pornographic material, fail to rewind a video before returning it to the video store, or illegally download music? We suspect not. Why? Because there are a variety of obstacles to getting accurate statistics for certain purposes, including unwillingness to provide truthful information, failure to report events, and physical barriers to observing events. Consequently, statistics are often in the form of "educated guesses." Such estimates can be quite useful; they can also be quite deceiving. Always ask, "How did the author arrive at the estimate?"

Confusing Averages

Examine the following statements:

> (1) One way to make money fast is to become a professional golfer. The average professional golfer made $874,840.23 in tournament earnings alone in 2004.

> (2) There is no reason to worry about the new nuclear power plant's being built in our city; the average amount of harm caused by nuclear accidents is rather low.

Both examples use the word "average." But there are three different ways to determine an average, and in most cases each will give you a different average. What are the three ways? One is to add all the values and divide this total by the number of values used. The result is the *mean*.

A second way is to list all the values from highest to lowest, then find the one in the middle. This middle value is the *median*. Half of the values will be above the *median*; half will be below it. A third way is to list all the values and then count each different value or range of values. The value that appears most frequently is called the *mode*, the third kind of average.

It makes a big difference whether a writer is talking about the mean, median, or mode. Think about the winning distribution in any professional sport. Some individuals win extremely high amounts from tournaments, and these people tend to win many tournaments. Such high winnings will increase the mean dramatically. They will have little effect, however, on either the median or the mode. Thus, if one wishes to make the average winnings seem high in this situation, the mean is probably the best average to present. For example, the highest golf winnings in 2004 was $10,905,166, substantially high enough to skew the mean. The median winnings in 2004 was $566,472, which is much lower than the mean. In fact, slightly over one-third of the golfers won sums above the mean. You should now be able to see how important it is to know which average is used when people talk about salaries or income.

Now, let's look carefully at example (2). If the average presented is either the mode or the median, we may be tricked into a false sense of security. For example, it is possible that many "small" accidents happen, causing very little damage. However, we would also want to know about larger accidents. How much damage is caused by these larger accidents, and how frequently do these larger accidents occur? These are all questions we would want to have answered before we feel secure with the new nuclear power plant. If there are a few very large accidents, but most are rather minor, the mode and the median nuclear accident values could be quite low, but the mean would be very high.

When you see "average" values, always ask: "Does it matter whether it is the mean, the median, or the mode?" To answer this question, consider how using the various meanings of average might change the significance of the information.

Not only is it important to determine whether an average is a mean, median, or mode, but it is often also important to determine the gap between the smallest and largest values—the range—and how frequently each of the values occurs—the distribution. For example, assume that you are at a casino and are trying to figure out which slot machine to play. Would you be satisfied with information about the average payout for each machine? We wouldn't.

We would want to know the range of payout, that is, the highest and the lowest cash winnings as well as the frequency of the different levels. The average might seem impressive, but if 15 percent of people end up losing all of their money without winning once, we suspect that you would rather do something else with your money. Also, if the frequency of payoff of high money amounts if very low, you might second guess your choice of slot machine.

Let's consider another example in which knowing the range and distribution would be important.

> Engaging in premarital sex is not as dangerous as many people would have you
> believe. Nationwide, fewer than eight percent of people who have premarital sex
> end up with a sexually transmitted disease.

First, we suspect that this statistic represents the mean. While the mean number of people contracting STDs through premarital sex may be quite low, there are probably areas across the country where this number is much higher or much lower than the mean. In a certain area the risk might not be high, but it is likely to be much higher in other areas of the country. It would probably be important to know the range and frequency of different STDs that people having premarital sex contract. If of those eight percent, 25 percent contract the HIV virus, you might not be so quick to believe the above argument's claim of the safety of premarital sex.

Thus, when an average is presented, ask yourself: "Would it be important for me to know the range and distribution of values?"

Concluding One Thing, Proving Another

Communicators often deceive us when they use statistics that prove one thing but then claim to have proved something quite different. The statistics don't prove what they seem to! We suggest two strategies for locating such deception.

One strategy is to *blind yourself to the communicator's statistics* and ask yourself, "What statistical evidence would be helpful in proving her conclusion?" Then, compare the needed statistics to the statistics given. If the two do not match, you may have located a statistical deception. The following example provides you with an opportunity to apply that strategy.

> A new weight-loss drug, Fatsaway, is effective in helping obese people lose weight.
> In a clinical trial, only 6 out of 100 people on Fatsaway reported any side effects with
> taking the drug. The company manufacturing the drug argues, "With 94 percent of
> people having positive results with Fatsaway, it is safe to say our pill is one of the most
> effective weight-loss pills in the market."

How should the company manufacturing the drug have proven its conclusion that Fatsaway is 94 percent effective as a weight-loss pill? Shouldn't they have performed a study as to how many people lost weight with the pill, and how much weight these people lost? Instead, the company reported statistics regarding the frequency of side effects and has assumed that if the pill did not produce side effects then the pill was effective in helping them lose weight. The company proves one thing (relatively small number of people report side effects with Fatsaway) and concludes another (Fatsaway is effective at helping people lose weight). An important lesson to learn from this example is to *pay close attention to both the wording of the statistics and the wording of the conclusion* to see whether they are referring to the same thing. When they are not, the author or speaker may be lying with statistics.

It is frequently difficult to know just what statistical evidence should be provided to support a conclusion. Thus, another strategy is to examine the author's statistics *very closely* while *blinding yourself to the conclusion*; then ask yourself, "What is the appropriate conclusion to be drawn from those statistics?" Then, compare your conclusion with the author's. Try that strategy with the following example.

> Almost half of all Americans cheat on their significant others. A researcher recently interviewed people at a shopping mall. Of the 75 people responding to the survey, 36 admitting to having cheated on someone they were "seeing."

Did you come up with the following conclusion? Almost half of the people *in one given location* admit to having cheated, *at least once*, on someone with whom they were dating or were otherwise involved. Do you see the difference between what the statistics proved and what the author concluded? If so, you have discovered how this author has lied with statistics.

Now, practice on the following.

> A recent survey asked college students, "Have you ever had a night of binge drinking during the school year?" The researcher reported that 83 percent of college students answer "yes" and concluded, "The results demonstrate that universities are overly stressing their students, causing the students to engage in dangerous drinking habits to escape the pressures of college classes."

Do you see how the writer has concluded one thing while proving another? Do you think the results might have been different if the researcher had asked, "Do you drink to escape the stress from your college classes?"

Deceiving by Omitting Information

Statistics often deceive us because they are incomplete. Thus, a further helpful strategy for locating flaws in statistical reasoning is to ask, "*What further information do you need before you can judge the impact of the statistics?*" Let's look at two examples to illustrate the usefulness of this question.

1. Large businesses are destroying the small town feel of our "downtown" area. Just last year, the number of large businesses in the city has increased by 75 percent.

2. Despite common fears, skydiving is much safer than other activities, such as driving a car. In one particular month, in Los Angeles, 176 people died in car accidents while 3 died in skydiving accidents.

In the first example, 75 percent seems quite impressive. But something is missing: The *absolute numbers* on which this percentage is based. Wouldn't we be less alarmed if we knew that this increase was from four businesses to seven, rather than from 12 to 21? In our second example, we have the numbers, but we don't have the *percentages*. Wouldn't we need to know what these numbers mean in terms of percentages of people involved in both activities? After all, there are fewer total skydivers than there are people traveling in cars.

When you encounter impressive-sounding numbers or percentages, be wary. You may need to get other information to decide just how impressive the numbers are. When only absolute numbers are presented, ask whether percentages might help you make a better judgment; when only percentages are presented, ask whether absolute numbers would enrich their meaning.

Another important kind of potential missing information is *relevant comparisons.* It is often useful to ask the question, "As compared to . . . ?"

Each of the following statements illustrates statistics that can benefit from asking for comparisons:

•   Medusa hair spray, now 50 percent better.

•   SUVs are dangerous and should not be allowed on the road. In 2004, SUVs were responsible for 4,666 deaths. Certainly something needs to be done.

•   Movie budgets are outrageous nowadays. Just look at *Star Wars: Revenge of the Sith*, the budget for that movie alone is $115,000,000!

With reference to the first statement, don't you need to ask, "50 percent better than what?" Other ineffective hair sprays? Previous Medusa brand hair spray? As for the second statement, wouldn't you want to know how many of those deaths would have been prevented if an SUV were not involved, how many other motor vehicle fatalities not involving an SUV there were, the number of SUVs on the road compared to how many deaths they were involved in, and how many miles SUVs travel compared to how many deaths occur in SUVs? With reference to the third statement, how does the budget of one particular movie relate to the budget of other movies, and is this one case highly unusual, or is it typical of the movie industry?

When you encounter statistics, be sure to ask, "What relevant information is missing?"

Risk Statistics and Omitted Information

> "Daily use of Nepenthe brand aspirin will lower the chance of a second heart attack by 55 percent."

> "Routine physicals have been linked to finding early cures and lowering people's likelihood of early death by 13 percent."

A common use of statistics in arguments—especially arguments about health risks—is the reporting of risk reduction as a result of some intervention. Such reports can be deceptive. The same amount of risk reduction can be reported in *relative* or *absolute* terms, and these differences can greatly affect our perceptions of the actual amount of risk reduction.

Imagine a 65-year-old woman who just had a stroke and is discussing treatment options with her doctor. The doctor quotes statistics about three treatment options:

(1) Treatment X will reduce the likelihood of a future stroke by 33 percent,

(2) Treatment Y will reduce the risk by three percent, and

(3) With treatment Z, 94 percent of women are free of a second stroke for 10 years, compared to 91 percent of those who go untreated.

Which treatment should she choose? Our guess is that she will choose the first. But all of these options refer to the same size treatment effect. They just express the risk in different ways. The first (the 33 percent) is the "relative risk reduction." If a treatment reduces the risk of heart attack from 9 in 100 to 6 in 100, the risk is reduced by one-third, or 33 percent. But the *absolute* change, from 9 to 6 percent, is only a three percent reduction, and the improvement of a good outcome from 91 to 94 is also only three percent. The point is that expressing risk reductions in relative, rather than absolute terms, can make treatment effects seem larger than they really are, and individuals are more likely to embrace a treatment when benefits are expressed in relative rather than absolute terms. As you might expect, drug companies usually use relative risk in their ads, and media reports also tend to focus on relative risk.

Relative risk reduction statistics can be deceiving. When you encounter arguments using such statistics, always try to determine how the results might be different and less impressive if expressed in absolute terms.

Summary

We have highlighted a number of ways by which you can catch people "lying" with statistics. We hope that you can now see the problem with statistic about the widespread use of the term "Kafkaesque." *Hints*: Where did that impressive figure of more than 250 languages come from? Have Kafka's works been translated into more than 250 languages?

Clues for Assessing Statistics

1. Try to find out as much as you can about how the statistics were obtained. Ask, *"How does the author or speaker know?"*
2. Be curious about the type of average being described.
3. Be alert to users of statistics *concluding one thing, but proving another.*
4. Blind yourself to the writer's or speaker's statistics and compare the needed statistical evidence with the statistics actually provided.
5. Form your own conclusion from the statistics. If it doesn't match the author's or speaker's conclusion, then something is probably wrong.
6. Determine what information is missing. Be especially alert for misleading numbers and percentages and for missing comparisons.

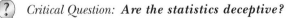 *Critical Question:* **Are the statistics deceptive?**

Practice Exercises

For each of the practice passages, identify inadequacies in the evidence.

Passage 1

Campaigns for national office are getting out of hand. Money is playing a central role in more and more elections. The average winner in a Senate race now spends over $8 million in his or her campaign, while typical presidential candidates spend more than $300 million. It is time for some serious changes, because we cannot simply allow politicians to buy their seats through large expenditures on advertisements.

Passage 2

The home is becoming a more dangerous place to spend time. The number of home related injuries is on the rise. In 2000, approximately 2,300 children aged 14 and under died from accidents in the home. Also, 4.7 million people are bit by dogs each year. To make matters worse, even television, a relatively safe household appliance is becoming dangerous. In fact, 42,000 people are injured by televisions and television stands each year. With so many accidents in the home, perhaps people need to start spending more time outdoors.

Passage 3

Looking fashionable has never been easier! Every year the number of fashion designers increases by 8 percent, making a wider selection of fashionable objects available. Also, because the price of fashionable merchandise reflects the status the clothing brings with it, it is very easy to pick out the most fashionable articles of clothing. Furthermore, the leading fashion magazines have improved in quality by 46 percent. Certainly anyone can look fashionable if he or she wishes to do so.

Sample Responses

Passage 1

CONCLUSION: *A change in campaigning for national office is necessary.*

REASON: *Politicians are spending too much on campaigns. The average Senator spent more than $8 million on his or her campaign. Presidential candidates spend more than $300 million on their campaigns.*

Are campaigns costing too much money? The word *average* and *typical* should alert us to a potential deception. We need to know the kind of average used for these statistics. Was it the mean, median, or the mode? For example, using the mean in the Senate race data could potentially lead to a figure that is skewed because of certain, particularly close, Senate races where candidates spent large sums of money. However, because many Senators are basically guaranteed re-election, these races probably involve less spending. We know that only a few Senate race elections are usually close. Therefore, most probably do not spend as much as was reported, if the mean was used to present the average. In other words, the median or the mode would probably show a lower value.

There are also important missing comparison figures. How does campaign spending compare to similar spending in the past? What about for other offices? It is possible that campaign spending has actually gone down in recent years.

Passage 2

CONCLUSION: *It is becoming increasingly dangerous to spend time in one's home.*

REASONS: 1. *Household-related injuries are on the rise.*
2. *In one year, 2,300 children died in household accidents.*
3. *4.7 million people are bit by dogs every year.*
4. 42,000 people are injured by televisions each year.

To evaluate the argument, we need to first determine what the most appropriate evidence is to answer the question, "Are households more unsafe than they used to be?" In our opinion, the best statistic to use to answer the preceding question is a comparison of the rate of serious household accidents per year now and the same statistic over the past. Also relevant is the number of injuries per hour spent in the house verses the same statistic for past years. It is possible that more household injuries occur because people are spending more time in their houses than they used to spend. If they are inside the house more, it is only logical that the number of injuries occurring in the house would also rise.

The evidence presented in the argument is questionable for a number of reasons. First, no number is given at all regarding the number of household injuries. We know the author says they are on the rise, but no evidence is provided demonstrating a rise. Second, no details are given regarding the deaths of children in household accidents. How does this statistic compare to children's deaths in the home in the past? What types of accidents are causing these children's deaths? Third, the number of dog bites is deceptive. We do not know whether these dog bites occur in the home. More importantly, the number of dog bites does not seem to move us toward the conclusion that being at home is unsafe. Fourth, the statistic regarding televisions is questionable. Where does the author get the impressive sounding statistic? Also, how serious are most of these injuries?

CRITICAL QUESTION SUMMARY:
WHY THIS QUESTION IS IMPORTANT

Are the Statistics Deceptive?

Authors often provide statistics to support their reasoning. The statistics appear to be hard evidence. However, there are many ways that statistics can be misused. Because problematic statistics are used frequently, it is important to identify any problems with the statistics so that you can more carefully determine whether you will accept or reject the author's conclusion.

CHAPTER

12

WHAT SIGNIFICANT
INFORMATION IS OMITTED?

How compelling are the following advertisements?

> Try Happyme, the number one doctor prescribed treatment for depression.

> See *Kingdom of Heaven*, the best action film of the year!

The purpose of the advertisements is, of course, to persuade you to buy more of the designated product and to see the designated movie. Even before your critical-thinking skills developed to their current level, you knew that such advertisements tell less than the whole truth. For example, if the Happyme Company gives a bigger discount to psychiatrists than do other pharmaceutical companies, provides psychiatrists with greater numbers of free samples, or provides cruises for psychiatrists who use their product, you are unlikely to see this information included in the ad. You will not see that information, but it is quite relevant to your decision about what to take for your depression.

While critical thinkers are seeking the strength of autonomy, they cannot do so if they are making decisions on the basis of highly limited information. Almost any conclusion or product has some positive characteristics. Those who have an interest in telling us only the information they want us to know will tell us all of these positive characteristics in great and vivid detail. But they will hide the negative aspects of their conclusions. Thus, actual autonomy requires our persistent searching for what is being hidden, either accidentally or on purpose.

By asking questions learned in previous chapters, such as those concerning ambiguity, assumptions, and evidence, you will detect much important missing information. This chapter tries to sensitize you even more to the importance of *what is not said* and to serve as an important reminder that we react to an incomplete picture of an argument when we evaluate only the *explicit* parts. We thus devote this chapter to an extremely important additional question you must ask to judge the quality of reasoning: What significant information is omitted?

(?)   *Critical Question:* **What significant information is omitted?**

The Benefits of Detecting Omitted Information

You should remember that almost any information that you encounter has a purpose. In other words, its organization was selected and organized by someone who hoped that it would affect your thinking in some way. Hence, your task is to decide whether you wish to be an instrument of the chosen purpose. Often that purpose is to persuade you.

Advertisers, teachers, politicians, authors, speakers, and parents all organize information to shape your decisions. It is a natural and highly predictable desire on their part. Thus, those trying to persuade you will almost always try to present their position in the strongest possible light. So when you find what you believe to be persuasive reasons—those gold nuggets for which you are prospecting—it's wise to hesitate and to think about what the author may *not* have told you, something that your critical questioning has not yet revealed.

By *significant omitted information,* we mean information that would affect whether you should be influenced by a speaker's or writer's arguments, that is, information that *shapes the reasoning!* Interspersed throughout the chapter will be examples of reasoning that is not very convincing, not because of what is said but because of what is omitted. Study the examples carefully and notice how in each case the failure to look for omitted information would have resulted in your making a premature and potentially erroneous judgment.

The Certainty of Incomplete Reasoning

Incomplete reasoning is inevitable for several reasons. First, there is the limitation imposed by time and space. Arguments are incomplete because communicators do not have forever to organize them, nor do they have unlimited space or time in which to present their reasons.

Second, most of us have a very limited attention span; we get bored when messages are too long. Thus, communicators often feel a need to get their message across quickly. Advertisements and editorials reflect both these factors. For example, editorials are limited to a specific number of words, and the argument must both be interesting and make the author's point. Editorial writers, therefore, engage in many annoying omissions. Television commentators are notorious for making highly complicated issues sound as if they are simple. They have very little time to provide the degree of accurate information that you will need to form a reasonable conclusion. So our minds need to do a lot of extra work to fill in the many gaps in what they have to say in these situations.

A third reason for the inevitability of missing information is that the knowledge possessed by the person making the argument will always be incomplete. A fourth reason why information may be omitted is because of an outright attempt to deceive. Advertisers *know* they are omitting key bits of information. If they were to describe all the chemicals or cheap component parts that go into their products, you would be less likely to buy them. Experts in every field consciously omit information when open disclosure would weaken the persuasive effect of their advice. Such omissions are particularly tempting if those trying to advise you see you as a "sponge."

A final important reason why omitted information is so prevalent is that the values, beliefs, and attitudes of those trying to advise or persuade you are frequently different from yours. You can expect, therefore, that their reasoning will be guided by different assumptions from those you would have brought to the same question. Critical thinkers value curiosity and reasonableness; those working to persuade you often want to extinguish your curiosity and to encourage you to rely on unreasonable emotional responses to shape your choices.

A particular perspective is like a pair of blinders on a horse. The blinders improve the tendency of the horse to focus on what is directly in front of it. Yet, an individual's perspective, like blinders on a horse, prevents that person from noting certain information that would be important to those who reason from a different frame of reference. Unless your perspective is identical to that of the person trying to persuade you, important omissions of information are to be expected.

Let's review. Omitted information is inevitable for at least five reasons.

1. time and space limitations;
2. limited attention span;
3. inadequacies in human knowledge;
4. deception; and
5. existence of different perspectives.

Questions that Identify Omitted Information

If you are now convinced that reasoning will necessarily be incomplete, you may ask, "What am I supposed to do?" Well, initially you have to remind yourself that regardless of how attractive the reasons supporting a particular decision or opinion may seem at first glance, it's necessary to take another look in search of omitted information.

How do you search, and what can you expect to find? You ask questions to help decide what additional information you need, and then ask questions designed to reveal that information.

Isn't it silly to ask questions of an author who cannot answer? Not at all! Although the writer won't answer your questions, asking him has positive results. First, you may be able to supply the missing information because of what you already know. Second, searching for omitted information in persuasive writing gives you good practice for when you are able to search for omitted information face-to-face with a teacher or anyone else who is trying to persuade you orally. Even more importantly, searching for missing information prevents you from making up your mind too soon. By asking such questions of written material, you are reminding yourself that the information provided is incomplete and that whatever conclusion you reach on the basis of incomplete information will necessarily be very tentative.

There are many different kinds of questions you can use to identify relevant omitted information. Some questions you have already learned to ask will highlight important omitted information. For example, asking critical questions about ambiguity, the use of evidence, and the quality of assumptions usually identifies relevant omitted information.

In addition, to help you determine omitted information that might get overlooked by other critical questions, we provide you below with a list of some important kinds of omitted information and some examples of questions to help detect them.

Clues for Finding Common Kinds of Significant Information

1. **Common counterarguments**
    a. What reasons would someone who disagrees offer?
    b. Are there research studies that contradict the studies presented?
    c. Are there missing examples, testimonials, or analogies that support the other side of the argument?

2. **Missing definitions**
    a. How would the arguments differ if key terms were defined in other ways?

3. **Missing value preferences or perspectives**
    a. Would different values create a different approach to this issue?
    b. What arguments would flow from values different from those of the speaker or writer?

4. **Origins of "facts" referred to in the argument**
    a. What is the source for the "facts?"
    b. Are the factual claims supported by competent research or by reliable sources?

5. **Details of procedures used for gathering facts**
    a. How many people completed the questionnaire?
    b. How were the survey questions worded?
    c. Did respondents have ample opportunity to provide answers different from those reported by the person using the responses?

6. **Alternative techniques for gathering or organizing the evidence**
    a. How might the results from an interview study differ from written questionnaire results?
    b. Would a laboratory experiment have created more reliable and informative results?

7. **Missing or incomplete figures, graphs, tables, or data**
    a. Would the data look different if it included evidence from earlier or later years?
    b. Has the author "stretched" the figure to make the differences look larger?

8. **Omitted effects, both positive and negative, and both short- and long-term, of what is advocated and what is opposed**
    a. Has the argument left out important positive or negative consequences of a proposed action?
    b. Do we need to know the impact of the action on any of the following areas: political, social, economic, biological, spiritual, health, or environmental?

9. **Context of quotes and testimonials**
    a. Has a quote or testimonial been taken out of context?
    b. Would a different context have stimulated divergent responses?

10. **Benefits accruing to the author from convincing others to follow her advice**
    a. Will the author benefit financially if we adopt her proposed policy?
    b. Does the author's career depend in some manner on a particular conclusion?

Being aware of these specific types should help you a lot in locating relevant omitted information. Because there are so many kinds of important omitted information, however, you should always ask yourself the general question, "Has the speaker or writer left out any other information that I need to know before I judge the quality of his reasoning?"

Let's examine some arguments that have omitted some of the types of information just listed and watch how each omission might cause us to form a faulty conclusion. Only by asking that omitted information be supplied in each case could you avoid this danger. Initially, let's look at an advertising claim.

Zitout brand facial cleanser's commercials claim that the cleanser removes 95 percent of deep-down dirt and oil, helping to fight unsightly blemishes. Should we all run out and buy Zitout facial cleanser? Wait just a minute! Among many omissions, the advertisement fails to include any of the following pieces of information: (a) what percentage of deep-down dirt and oil other facial cleansers remove; maybe they remove 99 percent of dirt and oil; (b) amount of dirt and oil removed by washing with soap alone; it might be possible that faces can be cleaned adequately with normal soap; (c) potential negative consequences of using this specific product; it is possible that some of the ingredients might cause excessive dryness or pose cancer risks; (d) other sources of blemishes; perhaps dirt and oil are not the highest concerns when washing one's face; (e) how much dirt and oil is necessary to cause blemishes; maybe five percent will still cause a significant number of blemishes; and (f) other advantages or disadvantages of the facial cleanser, such as smell, price, and length of effective action. The advertiser has omitted much significant data that you would need if you were to buy wisely.

Do you see how advertising phrases like "4 out of 5 doctors agree," "all natural," "fat free," "low in carbs," "good for your heart," "number 1 leading brand," "ADA approved," and "no added preservatives" may all be accurate but misleading because of omitted information?

It's pretty obvious that advertising omits much relevant information. Let's now take a look at a more complicated reasoning example. Read the following excerpt and ask yourself what has been omitted, referring to our list for clues to your search.

> A great way to keep a buzz going for longer is to mix energy drinks with alcohol. The energy from the drink allows you to party longer as the alcohol does not affect you as much as it would without the energy drink. Plus, the added stimulants in the energy drink keep you alert, preventing you from becoming impaired due to alcohol consumption. Studies have shown that people mixing energy

drinks with alcohol can party 65 percent longer. Also, energy drinks prevent hangovers, as surveys have shown that people who mix alcohol and energy drinks report 75 percent fewer hangovers than drinking alcohol alone causes, while maintaining a buzz 59 percent longer. Furthermore, Super Stim, a leading brand of energy drink, does not mention anything about negative health consequences on their website from mixing their drink with alcohol. Clearly, there is much good and no harm in mixing energy drinks and alcohol.

What important information do you need to know before you can decide whether mixing energy drinks and alcohol is helpful and safe? Let us suggest some questions.

What common counterarguments or counterexamples might doctors or other specialists use to refute this reasoning? We can imagine counterarguments highlighting that hangovers are a result of dehydration, and that caffeine, commonly found in large quantities in energy drinks, is a diuretic, also causing dehydration. Also, the stimulants will keep people alert, but do not prevent impairment, giving people a false sense of being more sober than they really are.

What are possible health risks associated with mixing stimulants and depressants? It is important to know that researchers at Ball State University have recently released statements saying the mixing of stimulants and depressants in energy drinks and alcohol respectively can cause cardiopulmonary and cardiovascular failures. What counts as an "energy drink?" What value assumptions does the argument contain that lead to an advocating of mixing energy drinks and alcohol?

What is the origin of the facts alluded to in the argument? How does the author know that people can party 65 percent longer, and people experience 75 percent fewer hangovers? Also, how confident can we be of the survey reports of fewer hangovers? We know nothing about the research cited. So we cannot judge the quality of the statistics provided.

For example, is it helpful to you to know that in numerous recent studies, researchers have demonstrated how mixing energy drinks can lead to increased heart and liver problems? It is also important to realize that there is little specific evidence on whether energy drinks are helpful or harmful, on their own, to one's health. We would certainly want to examine these other studies, as well as the ones cited in the passage, to better evaluate all of the evidence available regarding the mixing of energy drinks and alcohol.

Would other research methods give us a different view of the safety of mixing energy drinks and alcoholic beverages? Would survey data results differ from tests performed in a laboratory on the interactions of chemicals in energy drinks and alcohol? Would a double-blind study giving people various drinks involving mixes of alcohol, stimulants, or a placebo liquid accurately provide statistics on risks from mixing energy drinks and alcohol?

We also know nothing about the author. It is relevant to find out any possible associations the author has with energy drink companies or providers of alcohol as these connections might bias the research. Also, if the author is a doctor unattached to either energy drink or alcohol companies, this information might lend credibility to the author's claims. The author has presented us with a very incomplete picture. Unless you complete the picture, your decision about the safety of mixing energy drinks and alcohol will be very uninformed.

The Importance of the Negative View

There is one type of omitted information that we believe is so important to identify and so often overlooked that we want to specifically highlight it for you: the *potential negative effects* of actions being advocated, such as the use of a new medication, the building of a large new school, or a proposed tax cut. We stress the negative effects here because usually proposals for such action come into existence in the context of backers' heralding their benefits, such as greater reduction of a certain medical problem, better appearance, more leisure, more educational opportunities, increased length of life, and more and/or improved commodities. However, because most actions have such widespread positive *and negative* impacts, we need to ask:

- Which segments of society do *not* benefit from a proposed action? Who loses? What do the losers have to say about it?
- How does the proposed action affect the distribution of power?
- Does the action influence the extent of democracy in our society?
- How does a particular action affect how we view the world: What we think, how we think, and what we know and can know?
- What are the action's effects on our health?
- How does the action influence our relationships with one another? With the natural environment?
- Will the action have a slow, cumulative impact?

For each of these questions, we always also want to ask, "What are the potential *long-term negative effects* of the action?"

To illustrate the usefulness of asking these omitted-information questions, let's reflect upon the following question: What are some possible negative effects of building a large new school? Did you think of the following?

- *Destruction of the environment.* For example, would the building of a new school involve the removal of a wooded area? How would the local wildlife be affected by the potential loss of a habitat?

- *Shifts in quality of education provided.* What if the new school attracts skilled teachers or gifted students away from other schools? What if the new school absorbed a significant amount of the funds available to schools, depriving other schools of the same funds?

- *Effects of property values.* If the school does not do well in comparison with national standards, how will this affect the property values of the houses in the surrounding community?

- *Increased tax burden.* How would the new school be funded? If the new school is a public school, the opening of the new school could result in an increase in property taxes for the local community to help support the new school.

- *Prevention of other potentially helpful expansion.* Is it possible that the land used for the school would have better been used for some other new building? For example, what if there were plenty of schools, but not enough jobs in the neighborhood, would the land have been better used to build new businesses?

- *Increased demand for housing.* Is there enough housing available in the community to accommodate new teachers and families that desire access to the new school?

Questions such as these can give us pause for thought before jumping on the bandwagon of a proposed action.

Omitted Information That Remains Missing

Just because you are able to request important missing information does not guarantee a satisfactory response. It is quite possible that your probing questions cannot be answered. Do not despair! You did your part. You requested information that you needed to make up your mind; you must now decide whether it is possible to arrive at a conclusion without the missing informa-tion. We warned you earlier that reasoning is always incomplete. Therefore, to claim automatically that you cannot make a decision as long as information is missing would prevent you from ever forming any opinions.

USING THIS CRITICAL QUESTION

Once you have thought about the existence of missing information in an argument, what should you do? The first logical reaction is to seek the infor-mation. But usually you will encounter resistance. Your options as a critical thinker are to voice your displeasure with the argument in light of the miss-ing information, keep searching for the information that you require, or cautiously agree with the reasoning on the grounds that this argument is better than its competitors.

Missing Information and Your Own Writing and Speaking

When you communicate, you will necessarily omit some information that your audience needs. However, at the same time, your experience using this critical question as an evaluative tool should forewarn you that some information is especially important for a strong argument. When you write or speak, you show respect for your audience when you include specific information that you know in advance will assist them in deciding the merits of your reasoning.

For example, when you propose an action, think about potential, relevant counterarguments to what you are advocating and share those counterargu-ments with your audience. To do otherwise is to insult them. They know there are alternative perspectives. So, in the interest of your own integrity, be open about their existence.

(?) *Critical Question:* **What significant information is omitted?**

Practice Exercises

In each of the following examples, there is important missing information. Make a list of questions you would ask the person who wrote each passage. Explain in each case why the information you are seeking is important to you as you try to decide the worth of the reasoning.

Passage 1

Recent research has shown that eating and sleeping less can lead to a longer life. In laboratory experiments, rats fed a bare minimum and allowed to sleep much less than normal were found to be better able to recover from injuries and to live longer lives than rats that were fed plenty of food and slept a substantial amount. The researchers concluded that people, too, could benefit from less eating and sleeping and more physical activity.

Passage 2

Cloning technology can lead to many positive breakthroughs in the medical field. If we were to adequately develop cloning technology, there would no longer be a need for people to die because of a lack of organ donors. With cloning, researchers could artificially develop new organs for people in need of transplants. Plus, because these organs would be cloned from the person's own tissues, there would be no chance of their body rejecting the transplanted organ. The cloned organs can be made in bodies that lack a head, and thus would not involve a "death" in order to save a life. Another advantage of cloning is that it can help fight disease. Certain proteins produced by clones can be used to fight diseases such as diabetes, Parkinson's disease, and Cystic Fibrosis.

Passage 3

America is the policeman of the world. It is our job to go into countries that need our help and to watch over them. One effective way to limit the inter-actions we need to have with other countries is to encourage the development of democracy and free markets in these countries. After all, the modern Western democracies have not fought wars against one another, and they are all democratic with a free market structure. Furthermore, look at the easy transition Germany had when it was reunited. Democracy was installed and the formerly split West and East Germany came along just fine. In fact, the German economy did really well with the transition also. Germany currently has the third largest GDP of any country in the world, all because of democracy and capitalism.

Sample Responses

Passage 1

CONCLUSION: *People would benefit from eating and sleeping less.*

REASON: *Studies on rats have shown that when rats eat and sleep less, they recover from injuries better and live longer than other rats.*

Before we all start to cut back on our food intake and amount of sleep, we should re-evaluate the information provided leading to this conclusion. What are the counterarguments, for example? Is it possible that humans and rats differ too much to generalize from one to other about the effects of sleep? Also, how much longer did the rats that ate and slept less live, and how much faster did these same rats recover from injuries? Is it possible that the variance is small or insignificant? Did the rats suffer any negative effects from eating and sleeping less? Would the rats have lived longer and recovered faster if instead of sleeping and eating less they ate and slept far more than the other rats?

Furthermore, just what do we know about the testing procedures? Nothing at all! These are just a few of the questions we would want to ask before we relied on the information in this passage.

Passage 2

CONCLUSION: *Cloning can provide positive medical benefits.*

Reasons: 1. *Clones can be used for human transplants.*
          2. *Clones can be used to help combat certain diseases.*

First, we should note that this reasoning advocates pursuing a new technology—human cloning—and cites only its advantages. The writer omits possible disadvantages. We need to consider both advantages and disadvantages. What serious side effects might result from using cloned organs? Are cloned organs as stable as regular organs? What positive and negative effects might cloning technology have on human decision-making? Would people be less likely to take care of their bodies and their organs if they knew that new organs could be grown to replace their current ones? Would the availability of the technology lead people to misuse cloning to produce complete human clones for an insidious purpose? Would people clone themselves, helping add to the burden already placed on the Earth by the current population? The advantages of the procedure may well outweigh the disadvantages, but we need to be aware of both in judging the merits of the conclusion.

Furthermore, let's look at the missing information regarding the research. Did you notice that no research has been cited? In fact, the argument fails to tell us that no tests on human cloning have occurred in the United States. Therefore, all of the discussion on the benefits of cloning is hypothetical. Would actual research prove the hypothetical benefits to be possible? We do not know.

CRITICAL QUESTION SUMMARY:
WHY THIS QUESTION IS IMPORTANT

What Significant Information Is Omitted?

When an author is trying to persuade you of something, she often leaves out important information. This information is often useful in assessing the worth of the conclusion. By explicitly looking for omitted information, you can determine whether the author has provided you with enough information to support the reasoning. If she has left out too much information, you cannot accept the reasons as support for the conclusion. Consequently, you should choose to reject her conclusion.

13

WHAT REASONABLE CONCLUSIONS ARE POSSIBLE?

By this stage you should be better equipped to pan for intellectual gold—to distinguish stronger reasons from weaker ones.

Consider the following argument:

> Large corporations spend far too much time and money advertising to children. Children's programming is riddled with commercials trying to sell them the latest toy, telling the children they will not be happy unless they have it. The practice of advertising to children is horrendous and should be illegal. Advertising to children, who cannot critically evaluate the ads they see, puts a strain on parents to either say "no" to their children and have them get upset, or to give in to their children's demands, ultimately spoiling the children.

Should you urge your local congressman to criminalize advertisements to children? Suppose you checked the author's reasons and found them believable. Are there other conclusions that might be equally consistent with these reasons as the author's conclusion? The chapter summary will suggest several possible alternative conclusions.

Very rarely will you have a situation in which only one conclusion can be reasonably inferred. In an earlier chapter, we discussed the importance of rival causes. The point there was that there are different possible causal bases for a particular conclusion. This chapter, however, focuses on the alternative *conclusions* that are all possible outcomes from a single set of reasons.

Consequently, you must make sure that the conclusion you eventually adopt is the most reasonable and the most consistent with your value preferences. The recognition that the reasons could provide support for conclusions different from yours should heighten your interest in any further tests or studies that would help identify the best conclusion.

 Critical Question: **What reasonable conclusions are possible?**

Assumptions and Multiple Conclusions

Evidence attempting to support a factual claim or a group of strong reasons supporting a prescriptive conclusion can both be interpreted to mean different things. Reasons do not generally speak for themselves in an obvious way. As we have seen many times, conclusions are reached only after someone makes certain interpretations or assumptions concerning the meaning of the reasons.

If you make a different assumption concerning the meaning of the reasons, you will reach different conclusions. Because we all possess different levels of perceptual precision, frames of reference, and prior knowledge, we repeatedly disagree about which assumptions are preferable. We form different conclusions from reasons because our diverse backgrounds and goals cause us to be attracted to different assumptions when we decide to link reasons to conclusions.

Sometimes a writer or speaker will mention alternative conclusions that can be reached on the basis of the reasons he has presented. However, you will often have to generate possible alternatives. To perform this creative task, try to imagine what different assumptions might enable someone to jump from the reasons you have identified to another conclusion. Remember, *many* possible conclusions can be made on the basis of most sets of reasons. The next two sections will help you recognize the multiplicity of possible conclusions.

Dichotomous Thinking: Impediment to Considering Multiple Conclusions

Very few important questions can be answered with a simple "yes" or an absolute "no." When people think in black or white, yes or no, right or wrong, or correct or incorrect terms, they engage in *dichotomous thinking*. This type of thinking consists of assuming there are only two possible answers to a question that has multiple potential answers. This habit of seeing and referring to *both* sides of a question as if there are only two has devastatingly destructive effects on our thinking. By restricting the conclusions we consider to be only two, we are sharply reducing the robust possibilities that careful reasoning can produce.

We encountered dichotomous thinking earlier when we discussed the Either-or fallacy. This fallacy, and dichotomous thinking in general, damages reasoning by overly restricting our vision. We think we are finished after considering two optional decisions, thereby overlooking many options and the positive consequences that could have resulted from choosing one of them.

Dichotomous thinkers often are rigid and intolerant because they fail to understand the importance of context for a particular answer. To see this point more clearly, imagine this situation:

Your roommate asks you to help plan her biology paper. The paper is to address the question: Should scientists pursue stem cell research? In her mind, the paper requires her to defend a "yes" or "no" position.

You have learned that dichotomous thinking can be avoided by qualifying conclusions, by putting them into context. This qualification process requires you to ask about any conclusion:

1. *When* is it accurate?
2. *Where* is it accurate?
3. *Why* or *for what purpose* is it accurate?

You then begin to apply this process to the paper assignment.

Would you be surprised by your roommate's growing frustration as you explained that at certain specified times, in certain situations, to maximize particular values or objectives one should allow stem cell research? She's looking for "yes" or "no"; you provided a complicated "it depends on. . ."

Rigid, dichotomous thinking limits the range of your decisions and opinions. Even worse, it overly simplifies complex situations. As a consequence, dichotomous thinkers are high-risk candidates for confusion.

The next section illustrates the restrictive effects of dichotomous thinking.

Two Sides or Many?

Before we look at several arguments in which multiple conclusions are possible, let's make sure you appreciate the large number of conclusions that are possible with respect to most important controversies. Here are three contemporary questions.

1. Should the United States engage in peacekeeping in other countries?
2. Is William Shakespeare the best playwright of all time?
3. Should scientists be held responsible for how their inventions are used?

At first glance, these questions and many like them seem to call for yes or no answers. However, a qualified yes or no is often the best answer. The advantage of *maybe* as an answer is that it forces you to admit that you do not yet know enough to make a definite answer. But at the same time you avoid a definite answer; you form a tentative decision or opinion that calls for commitment and eventual action. It's wise to seek additional information that would improve the support for your opinions, but at some point you must stop searching and make a decision, even when the most forceful answer you are willing to defend is a "yes, but . . ."

Glance back at the three questions that preceded the last paragraph. Ask yourself what conclusions would be possible in response to each question. Naturally, a simple "yes" or a "no" answer would be two possible conclusions. Are there others? Yes, there are many! Let's look at just a few of the possible answers to the first of these questions.

Should the United States Engage in Peacekeeping in Other Countries?

1. Yes, when the country is intricately tied to the United States, such as Saudi Arabia.
2. Yes, if the United States is to be perceived as the sole superpower responsible for maintaining world peace.
3. Yes, if the United States' role is to be limited to keeping peace and does not involve actually fighting a war.
4. Yes, when our economic interests abroad are at stake.
5. Yes, when Americans might be harmed by violence in other countries.
6. No, the United States has enough domestic problems to handle such that we should not spend time in other countries.
7. No, if peacekeeping is the goal, such actions are better left up to the U.N. or NATO.

Notice that in each case we added a condition necessary before the conclusion can be justified. In the absence of any data or definitions, any of these seven conclusions could be most reasonable. These seven are just a few of the conclusions possible for the first question.

Just for practice, try to suggest five possible conclusions for the third question: Should scientists be held responsible for how their inventions are used?

Perhaps this conclusion occurred to you: Yes, if it can be demonstrated that the scientist had reason to suspect that the invention would be used in a way other than intended, to the detriment of other people. Or, maybe you thought of this one: No, if the purpose of science is understood to be the betterment of humankind, scientific research is then aimed at helping people, and it is not the fault of scientists if potentially beneficial inventions are misused by others. But probably neither of these appears on your list. Why are we so sure? Because there are an enormous number of possible conclusions for this question! It should be an unlikely coincidence if you had chosen either of these two from the huge list of possible conclusions. This greater number of answers is what we want you to grasp. Knowledge of the possibility of multiple conclusions will prevent you from leaping to one prematurely.

Searching for Multiple Conclusions

This section contains two arguments pointing out multiple conclusions that could be created from the reasons in each argument. The intention is to give you some models to use when you search for conclusions. In each case, we will give you the structure of the argument before we suggest alternative conclusions. Study the reasons without looking at the conclusion, and try to identify as many conclusions as possible that would follow from the reasons. You can always use the when, where, and why questions to help generate alternative conclusions.

> CONCLUSION: *The United States should continue to use the death penalty as a form of punishment.*
>
> REASONS: 1. *Without the death penalty, there is no way to punish people who commit wrongs, such as harming guards or inmates, after already having a life sentence.*
> 2. *It is only fair that someone should die for purposely taking the life of another.*

Let's start by accepting these reasons as sensible to us. What do we then make of them? We have one answer in the conclusion of the writer: Continue the use of the death penalty.

But even when we accept these two reasons, we would not necessarily conclude the same thing. Other conclusions make at least as much sense on the basis of this support. For example, it would follow that we should continue to use the death penalty, but only in cases where someone has already been sentenced to life in prison, and the prisoner kills a guard or another inmate.

Alternatively, these reasons might suggest that we need to maintain the death penalty in cases of prisoners' harming guards or other prisoners. Not only is this alternative conclusion logically supported by the reasons, but it also leads to a conclusion quite different from the original conclusion.

> CONCLUSION: *States need to allow people to end their lives when they feel their time has come.*
>
> REASONS: 1. *People have the right to choose when and how they want to die.*
> 2. *It is wrong to force people to stay alive, especially if they are suffering.*
> 3. *If ending one's life were legal, the government could regulate it more closely, allowing doctors to supervise suicides and administer pills to make the act quick and painless.*

What conclusions are possible? One would be to decriminalize suicide in one location and observe the ways in which the law is used and to what extent people avail themselves of the opportunity. Alternatively, the government could restrict the legalized suicides to cases where people are terminally ill and suffering. Another possibility based on a strong devotion to collective responsibility would be to allow the suicides, but only after the person went through a thorough counseling program to see if there was any way besides death that the person could find happiness. Observe that all three of these conclusions are possible even if we accept the truth of the three reasons. Thus, the same reasons frequently can be used to support several different conclusions.

Productivity of If-Clauses

If you went back over all the alternative conclusions discussed in this chapter, you would notice that each optional conclusion is possible because we are missing certain information, definitions, assumptions, or the frame of reference of the person analyzing the reasons. Consequently, we can create multiple conclusions by the judicious use of *if-clauses*. In an if-clause, we state a condition that we are assuming in order to enable us to reach a particular conclusion. Notice that the use of if-clauses permits us to arrive at a conclusion without pretending that we know more than we actually do about a particular controversy.

When you use if-clauses to precede conclusions, you are pointing out that your conclusion is based on particular claims or assumptions about which you are uncertain. To see what we mean, look at the following sample conditional statements that might precede conclusions.

1. If the tax cut is targeted towards those at the lower end of the economic spectrum, then . . .

2. If a novel contains an easily identifiable protagonist, a clear antagonist, and a thrilling climax, then . . .

3. If automakers can make cars that are more fuel efficient, then . . .

If-clauses present you with multiple conclusions that you should assess before making up your mind about the controversy, and they also broaden the list of possible conclusions from which you can choose your own position.

Alternative Solutions as Conclusions

We frequently encounter issues posed in the following form:

> Should we do X?
> Is X desirable?

Such questions naturally "pull" for dichotomous thinking. Often, however, posing questions in this manner hides a broader question, "What should we do about Y?" (usually some pressing problem). Rewording the question in this way leads us to generate multiple conclusions of a particular form: solutions to the problem raised by the reasons. Generating multiple solutions greatly increases the flexibility of our thinking.

Let's examine the following passage to illustrate the importance of generating multiple solutions as possible conclusions.

> Should we close the bars downtown? The answer is a resounding yes! Since the bars opened, a dozen young college students have suffered from alcohol poisoning.

Once we change this question to, "What should we do about the number of college students suffering from alcohol poisoning?" a number of possible solutions come to mind, which help us formulate our conclusion to the issue. For example, we might conclude: "No, we should not close the bars downtown; rather, we should strictly enforce the drinking age and fine bars that sell alcoholic beverages to minors."

When reasons in a prescriptive argument are statements of practical problems, look for different solutions to the problems as possible conclusions.

Clues for Identifying Alternative Conclusions

1. Try to identify as many conclusions as possible that would follow from the reasons.
2. Use *if-clauses* to qualify alternative conclusions.
3. Reword the issue to "What should we do about Y?"

The Liberating Effect of Recognizing Alternative Conclusions

If logic, facts, or studies were self-explanatory, we would approach learning in a particular manner. Our task would be to have someone else, a teacher perhaps, provide the beliefs that we should have. Specifically, we would seek that single identifiable set of beliefs that logic and facts dictate.

While we have tremendous respect for logic and facts, we cannot exaggerate their worth as guides for conclusion formation. They take us only so far; then we have to go the rest of the way toward belief, using the help that facts and logic have provided.

A first step in using that help is the search for possible multiple conclusions consistent with logic and the facts as we know them. This search liberates us in an important way. It frees us from the inflexible mode of learning sketched above. Once we recognize the variety of possible conclusions, each of us can experience the excitement of enhanced personal choice.

All Conclusions Are Not Created Equal

We want to warn you that the rewarding feeling that often comes with generating multiple conclusions may tempt you to treat them as equally credible and to believe your job is done after you've made your list. But remember that some conclusions can be better justified than others, and the most believable ones should be the ones that most affect your reaction to the author's reasoning. Indeed, one clever way to weaken strong reasoning about global warming or the cause of the war in Iraq or the wisdom of distance learning is to make the claim that experts disagree.

The implication of such a statement is that once disagreement is identified, one argument is as good as the next. Therefore, there is no basis for new action to address the problem. But such an approach is insulting to careful critical thinking. Critical thinkers have standards of careful reasoning that they can apply to identify the strongest reasoning.

Summary

Very rarely do reasons mean just one thing. After evaluating a set of reasons, you still must decide what conclusion is most consistent with the best reasons in the controversy. To avoid dichotomous thinking in your search for the strongest conclusion, provide alternative contexts for the conclusions through the use of when, where, and why questions.

Qualifications for conclusions will move you away from dichotomous thinking. If-clauses provide a technique for expressing these qualifications.

For instance, let's take another look at the argument for restricting advertisements aimed at children at the beginning of the chapter. What alternative conclusions might be consistent with the reasons given?

AUTHOR'S CONCLUSION: *Advertisements aimed at children should be illegal.*

ALTERNATIVE CONCLUSIONS: 1. *If corporations are to be treated as persons, then they have a right to free speech that includes advertisements; thus, their right to advertise should not be limited.*

2. *If it can be demonstrated that children are unable to assess what they view, and thus are heavily influenced by the advertisements they see, then advertisements aimed at children should be illegal.*

3. *If the purpose of the proposed legislation is to limit the content of advertisements aimed at children, then the government should not make such ads illegal, but rather take a more proactive role in regulating the content of advertisements aimed at children.*

Many additional alternative conclusions are possible in light of the author's reasons. We would shrink the quality of our decision making if we did not consider those alternative conclusions as possible bases for our own beliefs.

Practice Exercises

(?) *Critical Question:* ***What reasonable conclusions are possible?***

For each of the following arguments, identify different conclusions that could be drawn from the reasons.

Passage 1

Feeding large numbers of people is not easy. However, dining halls on campus should try to accommodate a larger variety of tastes. Students all across campus consistently complain not only about the quality of food, but the lack of selection they find in the dining halls. All the dining halls need to do is offer a wider range of food to better please more students, and thus keep more of them eating on campus as opposed to off campus. Dining services is failing its duty to the students when it does not provide a large selection of food options every day.

Passage 2

I have never been that strong of a runner, but when I bought my new training shoes, Mercury, my time greatly improved. Now I can run faster, longer, and am less sore afterward. *Runner's Digest* also says the Mercury is one of the best shoes on the market. Therefore, all people who want to run should buy Mercury shoes.

Passage 3

Many people feel it is a good idea to legalize prostitution. A substantial number of people visit prostitutes now even though the practice is generally illegal. So proponents argue that it makes sense to legalize prostitution. Are these people right? Absolutely not! Prostitution is a horribly immoral practice and it should not be legalized. Prostitution helps spread sexually transmitted infections. Also, the legalization of prostitution will cause more men to cheat on their wives with prostitutes with the consequent negative fallout for families. Nothing good could possibly come from the legalization of prostitution.

Sample Responses

Passage 1

CONCLUSION: *Dining services are not doing an adequate job of providing food on campus.*

Reasons: 1. *Students are upset about the quality of the food.*
           2. *There are not enough options provided every day.*
           3. *More options would keep students happy and keep them eating on campus.*

To work on this particular critical-thinking skill, we need to assume that the reasons are strong ones. If we accept these reasons as reliable, we could also reasonably infer the following conclusions:

If dining services' goal is to provide a wide selection of food while ensuring the least amount of wasted food at the end of the day, then they are not letting students down with the current selections offered to students.

If dining services aim to keep the price of on-campus food down, and a more expansive menu would cause an increase in prices, they are not failing in their duty to students.

Notice that the alternative conclusions put dining services in quite a different light compared to the negative portrayal they received in the original conclusion.

Passage 2

CONCLUSION: *All potential runners should buy Mercury brand shoes.*

REASON: 1. *When the author bought Mercury brand shoes, her time greatly improved.*
           2. Runner's Digest *stated that Mercury brand shoes are some of the best running shoes on the market.*

On the basis of these reasons, we could infer several alternative conclusions:

Runners who are similar to the author should buy Mercury brand running shoes.

If one can afford Mercury brand shoes, the shoes are a great resource for people who are trying to run faster and longer.

If a runner is unhappy with the shoes she currently uses for training, then she should buy Mercury brand running shoes.

CRITICAL QUESTION SUMMARY: WHY THIS QUESTION IS IMPORTANT

What Reasonable Conclusions Are Possible?

When you are deciding whether to accept or reject an author's conclusion, you want to make sure that the author has come to the most reasonable conclusion. An author often oversteps his reasoning when he comes to a conclusion. By identifying alternative reasonable conclusions, you can determine which alternative conclusions, if any, you would be willing to accept in place of the author's conclusion. This step is the final tool in deciding whether to accept or reject the author's conclusion.

14

PRACTICE AND REVIEW

In this chapter, we put it all together. We begin by again listing the critical questions. This checklist should serve as a handy guide for you until the questions become second nature. When you encounter articles, lectures, debates, textbooks, commercials, Internet messages, or any other materials relating to an important issue, you will find it useful to go through the checklist and check off each question as you ask and answer it.

Next we apply the critical questions by critically evaluating one position on a particular controversy. The major purpose of this discussion is to provide an example of a coherent application of all the critical-thinking steps.

We suggest that you follow the discussion with several goals in mind. You can treat it as a check on your understanding of previous chapters. Would you have asked the same questions? Would you have formed similar answers? Do you feel better able to judge the worth of someone's reasoning?

Question Checklist for Critical Thinking

1. What are the issue and the conclusion?
2. What are the reasons?
3. Which words or phrases are ambiguous?
4. What are the value conflicts and assumptions?

5. What are the descriptive assumptions?

6. Are there any fallacies in the reasoning?

7. How good is the evidence?

8. Are there rival causes?

9. Are the statistics deceptive?

10. What significant information is omitted?

11. What reasonable conclusions are possible?

Asking the Right Questions: A Comprehensive Example

We first present a passage that summarizes one position with respect to whether states should impose taxes to ensure that individuals maintain good health. This section is followed by a lengthy discussion based on all 11 critical-thinking questions.

> Self-discipline seems to be extraordinarily difficult for us. One area in which we see this lack of self-discipline is health, specifically with diet and exercise. People too often lack motivation to exercise on a regular basis. Although individuals typically think of exercise as a private matter, they are generally not aware of the consequences of their apathy on the well-being of others. If people were more aware of the detrimental effects that their not exercising has on themselves and on other people as well, perhaps they would be more motivated to visit the gym.
>
> But they are not. Hence, we need something more than an appeal to self-discipline to encourage healthy behavior. To fulfill this need, states should be permitted to impose taxes on individuals, primarily those who are seriously overweight or obese, for their failure to comply with state-mandated exercise and dieting programs.
>
> Statistics show that only 3 out of 10 people exercise regularly. Unfortunately, these individuals who do not exercise, in combination with their unhealthy eating habits, have a higher risk of developing certain life-threatening illnesses, like heart attacks, strokes, cancer, and diabetes. For instance, a diet that is high in fat and cholesterol leads to a buildup in the arteries, potentially causing a heart attack when the buildup occurs in an artery carrying blood to the heart, or causing a stroke when the buildup restricts blood flow to the brain.
>
> Similarly, exercise forces your heart to pump more blood, increasing your body's efficiency and possibly reducing the bad cholesterol in your body that could clog your arteries. But those persons who neglect healthier food and regular exercise run a higher risk of developing these kinds of diseases. Regular exercise and

a healthy diet could also reduce the risk of prostate cancer and Type 2 diabetes, as individuals who maintain a high-fiber diet could slow prostate cancer cell growth by 30%, and individuals who reduce their sugar consumption also reduce their likelihood of acquiring Type 2 diabetes.

But beyond the physical benefits of regular exercise and a good diet, individuals also are more likely to experience better mental acuity when they adopt a healthier lifestyle. Brain research suggests that demanding exercise produces greater numbers of nerve cells, which may enhance memory skills. This benefit of better mental acuity due to exercise extends to the entire community, in that the community is less likely to have a need to care for unhealthy individuals who lack the mental capacity to care for themselves. Furthermore, experts say that another benefit of exercise is that exercise reduces anxiety and stress.

Compare the consequences of poor diet and infrequent exercise on the community with a nation's budget. Just as a person gains weight by taking in more calories than they burn, a nation incurs a greater deficit when spending exceeds what a nation produces. But a government's spending, even when there is a large deficit, does affect not only the government, but the entire nation, just as an unhealthy person, who consumes too much and does not burn many calories, affects the community as well as the individual, while effectively running a "health deficit."

Consider some of the statistics related to obesity, which is caused by a lack of exercise and poor dieting. One recent study found that states are paying $75 billion to treat obesity, indicating that expenditures for obesity are approaching spending levels for treatment of smoking-related illnesses. Because states are using so much money to pay for obesity-related treatments, states are less able to use these limited resources to fund other programs, like services under Medicare and Medicaid. For example, 15.7 percent of California's Medicaid spending is used to treat obesity, meaning that those funds could be used to treat other diseases like most cancers, physical and mental disabilities, and common viral infections. In addition, obesity, unlike many other illnesses, is largely preventable, as individuals suffering from obesity could easily alter their unhealthy condition with regular exercise and a more nutritious and well-balanced diet.

Furthermore, a state tax on individuals who do not regularly exercise and diet would offer an additional source of funding to assist with treatment of obesity-related illnesses because there could be funding for additional research and development to prevent and treat obesity. But supposing these funds were not used to treat obesity-related diseases, they could then be applied in areas outside of healthcare, to pay for educational and social programs, police and fire divisions, or homeland security. Therefore, states, along with communities in general, have a responsibility to encourage healthy lifestyles.

When we consider that many individuals seemingly lack the motivation to exercise and properly diet, the state has every right to intervene, specifically by imposing a sort of health tax on those who do not comply with state exercise and dieting standards. Although this practice may seem somewhat discriminatory, it remains a fact that states and communities in general end up paying for most obesity-related treatments, and a state tax becomes the necessary alternative to individuals' inability to make careful decisions about exercise and diet.

What Are the Issue and the Conclusion?

The issue addressed in the previous passage is a prescriptive one: Should states be permitted to tax citizens who fail to meet exercise and dieting requirements? We know that this is the issue because of what the author seeks to prove. The author's reasons all support the conclusion that yes, states have the right to tax individuals who do not meet exercise and dieting requirements. The reasons emphasize problems for the community from a lack of exercise and proper nutrition of individuals, while highlighting the futility in our relying on individuals to alter their own behavior for the public good.

What Are the Reasons?

Let's paraphrase the reasons that lead to the conclusion that states should impose taxes on individuals who do not comply with exercise and dieting standards.

1. Most people lack motivation to alter their behavior to benefit the community.
2. Individuals' not exercising and eating well increases the risk of developing life-threatening diseases.

   Supporting reason: Heart attacks, strokes, cancer, and diabetes are associated with infrequent exercise and a poor diet.
3. Proper exercise promotes mental acuity, and this effect frees up caretaker time needed for those lacking self-care ability.

   Supporting reason: Brain research suggests that demanding exercise builds nerve cells, which helps memory.
4. People who exercise experience less stress and anxiety.

5. Obesity has resulted in high levels of state spending.

    Supporting reason: People who do not exercise or eat a nutritious diet are more likely to be obese.

    Supporting reason two: State spending to treat obesity-related diseases is approaching levels to treat illnesses related to cigarette smoking.

6. Diseases and problems related to poor dieting and exercise are largely preventable.

7. A state tax would provide funding for treatment of obesity and research to help prevent obesity.

8. Money spent on treating diseases related to obesity could be used elsewhere.

What Words or Phrases Are Ambiguous?

We look first for possible ambiguity that might weaken the reasoning presented by focusing on the author's major reasons. An important ambiguity pervades the entire argument. What precisely is meant by "regular exercise?"

The phrase may appear clear, but it could be interpreted in several different ways. Notice how your reaction to the author's emphasis on regular exercise would be affected by the choice of either of the following alternative definitions of regular exercise.

A. Weightlifting 3–4 days each week.

B. Participating in 30 minutes of cardiovascular exercise four days each week.

C. Spending three hours in the gym Monday through Friday.

If you believe, for example, that individuals should exercise only three days every week, you may be less supportive of the conclusion if the writer means the third definition. You might believe that such a stringent exercise routine would place undue hardship upon an individual and his or her family, as people would possibly spend more time in the gym than with their families.

In addition, the passage does not specify who should regularly exercise. Does the author think that all adults must regularly exercise, or only adults older than 40 who have a higher risk of developing certain illnesses? Child obesity is arguably a growing problem. Would the author recommend that children regularly exercise or else be taxed as well?

Clearly, we might agree or disagree with the conclusion depending on the meaning of regular exercise; thus the phrase is an important ambiguity.

The fourth reason includes another important ambiguity—stress and anxiety. Our willingness to see this reason as strongly supporting the conclusion will depend on our sense of the kind, frequency, and severity of such stress and anxiety.

What are the Value Conflicts and Assumptions?

The essay presents an interesting study in value conflicts. To appreciate these value conflicts, you must first uncover a value assumption necessary for the issue to even be phrased as it is. Before debating whether states should tax people for failing to exercise and diet according to state standards, we should realize that to some extent exercise and dieting is a matter of individual preference. Some individuals choose to exercise, while others rarely, if ever, exercise or diet. The author of the passage values the right of the individual to make choices on some level. But on another level, the author seems quite willing to put autonomy on hold for this particular issue.

The individual's right to choose conflicts with another underlying value: Collective responsibility. The argument for states' imposing a kind of health tax rests on the notion that states have a collective responsibility to ensure that individuals exercise and diet for the benefit of the community. The author suggests that behavior not be primarily based on what individuals believe to be in their best interest, but suggests that individual behavior should be based on that which is beneficial to the entire community. Thus, a value preference for collective responsibility over individual responsibility clearly influences the author's choice of reasons and conclusion.

Another value priority can be detected by linking the first and sixth reasons to the conclusion. Cooperation is favored over autonomy and comfort. Suggesting that individuals meet state-established goals of exercise and dieting reflects a preference for a certain means toward meeting these goals, viz., cooperation through state action. Cooperation conflicts with individuals' rights to make decisions about their own bodies and lifestyles. Such an approach places autonomy and comfort lower in our value priorities in the hope that diseases would be more frequently prevented.

What Are the Descriptive Assumptions?

For the first reason, if true, to support the conclusion, it is necessary to assume that the state tax will provide sufficient motivation for individuals to modify their behavior. This descriptive assumption is questionable. It is quite possible that many individuals will be so upset by state-sanctioned exercise and dieting programs that those who are overweight, and perhaps even those individuals who regularly exercise, would engage in widespread civil disobedience, avoiding exercise and refusing to pay the new tax. Implicit in the passage is a view of individuals as rational in the sense that they would respond to monetary incentives in the form of tax savings to live a healthier lifestyle. If we believe this may not be the case, then we are likely to question the degree to which this reason supports the conclusion.

A second significant descriptive assumption underlies the author's claims that obesity is linked to numerous diseases and mental problems. For these reasons to be supportive of the conclusion, the author is assuming that compliance with the state exercise and dieting program will reduce the number of instances of obesity-related diseases. However, the author does not provide substantial evidence to justify this assumption, making this descriptive assumption questionable.

Another descriptive assumption important to the argument is related to the eighth reason. The truth of this reason depends on the assumption that money not spent on obesity-related treatments will be used effectively in other programs, such as police and fire departments, homeland security, and education. In other words, this money will be used to strengthen these other programs. However, if we doubt the likelihood that money saved from obesity-related treatments would be effectively used in other programs that we deem important, we would be less likely to support the conclusion that states should place a tax on individuals if they fail to regularly exercise and diet.

Are There Any Fallacies in the Reasoning?

Several fallacies seriously damage the argument. First, the author diverts our attention from the real issues by using emotional language. Phrases like "consequences of their apathy," "detrimental effects," "life-threatening illnesses," and "health deficit," for example, create a negative emotional association to obesity. Also, phrases like "largely preventable" and "nutritious and well-balanced diet" tend to be positive buzz words that create a positive association to the author's position. This tactic diverts our attention from the larger issue and from specific, relevant reasons, such as advantages and disadvantages of state laws that regulate exercise and diet.

Second, the argument includes the False Dilemma fallacy. The first reason suggests that individuals lack discipline to regularly exercise and maintain a healthy diet. The author also mentions that "a state tax becomes the necessary alternative to individuals' making decisions about exercise and diet." For this statement to be true, the author must assume that there are only two choices: either individuals make decisions about their exercise and health in such a way that individuals and the community benefit from improving health, or the state must create a health program and tax those who fail to comply. Obviously, these are not the only alternatives to the issue. Other solutions are possible, as you will see when we discuss alternative conclusions.

How Good Is the Evidence?

First, we ask the question, is there *any* evidence for the claims? There is. Then, we should ask, what *kinds* of evidence does the author provide? The author cites several research studies, an analogy, and an appeal to authority as evidence. A close look at the evidence reveals a lack of *good* evidence.

The governmental spending analogy in the fourth paragraph is offered as evidence that individuals' choosing not to exercise affects the entire community. Relevant similarities exist between a governmental body making decisions about spending and an individual's decision about her health, such as the desirability of making careful decisions that take others' interests into account.

The differences, however, weaken the value of the analogy as evidence. One relevant difference relates to the author's comparison of one part to the whole. The author argues that an individual affects the community as a government affects the nation. However, in the former situation, an individual is a part of a community, which is composed of numerous individuals. But a government is not similar, in the sense that a nation is not made up of numerous governments, but numerous citizens. The analogy fails to consider that in one case two similar entities are being compared, while the other situation involves two distinctly different entities. A second major difference is the role that the smaller entity plays in each situation. Individuals typically do not make decisions about health on the basis of potential consequences to the community, regardless of how much the author believes people should; however, governments at minimum operate with the rhetoric of public interest in the forefront of their discussions. A third difference is that at times governmental decisions, such as running a deficit for several years, could be beneficial for a nation that was experiencing unemployment and needed additional spending to stimulate job creation. However, the author would seemingly not agree that being obese for several years could be beneficial to a community.

The third reason points to brain research as evidence that exercise enhances mental acuity. This information is weak, however, because information about the research is lacking, leaving important questions unanswered.

What is the source of this research? How many times have these kinds of studies been replicated? How many individuals in these studies were tested? Were the tests of mental acuity given to a random sample, involving individuals of various backgrounds, ages, health conditions, etc.? Without a more detailed description of the cited brain research, such research cannot be considered as helpful evidence.

Similarly, the author's appeal to expert testimony in the fourth reason as evidence that exercise reduces stress and anxiety suffers from a lack of important information. The author provides no reference to the study or how frequently these kinds of studies have been replicated. In addition, the author does not describe the ways in which the studies were conducted. Consider, for example, the possible differences in results from experts' testing the stress levels of a group of retirees in one study from parents who have multiple jobs in another study.

Are There Rival Causes?

Support for the fifth reason is based on the association between exercise and obesity, implying that a lack of the former causes the latter. But correlation does not prove causation! Rival causes can explain the relationship. For example, individuals who have a very low metabolism are more likely to be obese, regardless of their level of physical activity. Genetics could pre-dispose certain individuals to be obese, even though these individuals might exercise regularly.

Are the Statistics Deceptive?

Some of the statistics deceive us by proving one thing while concluding another. For example, the author of the passage describes the number of individuals who do not exercise regularly. The statistic that 3 out of 10 people exercise regularly, however, proves only that of those people surveyed 3 out of 10 exercise regularly. It certainly does *not* prove that 7 out of 10 also have a poor diet and are at a higher risk for developing life-threatening diseases. In fact, the statistic tells us nothing about dieting or risk of developing diseases.

Also, the statistic that people who maintain a high-fiber diet could slow prostate cell growth by 30% is obviously meant to illustrate one particular benefit of a high-fiber diet. But this statistic in its strongest form proves only that individuals who consume high amounts of fiber could slow the growth of prostate cancer by 30%, *not* that they are 30% less likely to develop some form of prostate cancer. In addition, this statistic says nothing about the role of exercise in the development of prostate cancer, nor does the statistic mention any other ways in which a healthy diet, apart from consuming large amounts of fiber, contributes to the likelihood of slowing prostate cancer cell growth. Important missing information about the role of exercise and diet in general is needed to substantiate the author's claim that exercise and diet reduce the risk of prostate cancer.

What Significant Information Is Omitted?

Because this argument, like nearly all arguments, has incomplete reasoning, the amount of information omitted is enormous. To sort through the passage's unanswered questions, you should focus on the most significant of the omitted information.

First, we should ask whether the author has provided reasons for why we should reject common counterarguments. For example, what reasons would someone provide who disagrees with the author's conclusion? The author does not discuss reasons why others might disagree with her reasoning. But were we to be more familiar with these common counterarguments, perhaps we would react differently to the author's reasoning.

Specific information about the association between exercise and dieting with mental acuity and stress would be helpful in the third and fourth reasons. In addition, interviews with people of various ages and backgrounds might suggest hypotheses about the impact of state laws that regulate exercise and diet.

Also, the author fails to consider the potential negative effects of allowing states to tax individuals who do not exercise and diet according to state standards. One such effect of states' regulating health is the possibility that exercise and eating, which are typically regarded as leisure activities, will be viewed largely as a means of avoiding punishment by taxation. In other words, instead of states' touting the importance of exercise and dieting for their benefits to health and the enjoyment of these leisure activities, the primary benefit might become avoidance of the health tax, nullifying many of the reasons for why people now choose a healthy lifestyle. Another possible negative effect is that state governments will have difficulty in monitoring individuals' exercise and dieting patterns. To implement this law effectively, states may spend more money on monitoring individuals than they are accumulating through increased taxes and healthcare savings from fewer treatments. Because the cost of healthcare for obesity-related treatments is such a significant reason in the author's argument, any evidence that might suggest that states would need to spend large amounts of money to apply the health law would make us seriously question the author's reasoning.

Another potential negative effect is more long term. The implementation of these laws might open the floodgates for more infringement on the rights of individuals. The argument is a classic one: If rights can be curbed in one instance, then why not this or that instance? The commonality of the argument should not, however, dissuade us from considering its validity. If the reasoning for health laws is found acceptable and similar reasoning is applied to other issues, then it is very probable that the reasoning will be accepted again. Before becoming a proponent for this or any argument, you should carefully consider the potential long-term effects of the action.

What Reasonable Conclusions Are Possible?

Let's first list the reasons that we were least able to criticize—recognizing that all of the reasoning has some flaws. Next we will identify alternative conclusions consistent with these reasons.

1. Individuals' not exercising and eating well increases their risk of developing life-threatening diseases.
2. Obesity has resulted in high levels of state spending.

Remember that we are looking for conclusions other than the one provided by the author that are reasonable, given the most compelling reasons.

One alternative conclusion that is consistent with both strong reasons is that communities could develop programs to educate the people within their communities about the importance of exercise and nutrition. Perhaps these educational programs would make people more aware of the increased risks associated with a lack of exercise and nutrition and would encourage others to visit the gym, thereby reducing the amount of spending needed to treat obesity. Another plausible conclusion is that states could limit how much they spend on obesity-related illnesses. Such limitations might increase the likelihood that individuals would respond by adopting a healthier lifestyle, realizing that states will not pay for treatments of diseases that are linked to obesity, particularly if conditions of obesity could have been mitigated by exercise and nutrition.

If people lack motivation to exercise due in part to limited access to expensive gyms with a large variety of equipment, classes, and trainers, then another possible alternative conclusion is that states should open gyms that provide cheaper access to the public, especially for individuals of higher health risks.

Our critical discussion responds to only some of the facets of the controversy over whether states should tax people who do not exercise and eat well. You may focus on other parts of the argument. Ultimately, if you care about this issue, you must decide which of the inferences to support. Critical thinking can take you only so far. The final step is yours.

You can feel relatively confident that after following our question checklist, you have asked the right questions about the arguments and you are well prepared to form a reasoned opinion of your own about the quality of the author's reasoning. To reach your own decision on this issue, we recommend that you seek out more relevant information and choose the reasons and values that are most consistent with what you know and what you care about.

Final Word

Critical thinking is a tool. It does something for you. In serving this function for you, critical thinking can perform well or not so well. We want to end the book by urging you to get optimal use of the attitudes and skills of critical thinking that you have worked so hard to develop.

The Tone of Your Critical Thinking

As a critical thinker, you have the capability to come across like an annoying warrior, constantly watching for ways to slay those who stray from careful reasoning. But learning is, in important ways, a social activity. We need one another for development; we need one another to share conversation and debate. None of us is so gifted that we can stand alone in the face of the complexities we encounter. Critical thinking can make you more self-reliant if you use it to improve your own decision-making.

Hence, critical thinkers need to think about what they are giving off when they use their critical thinking. When you use your critical thinking, you are sending some kind of message to others about what critical thinking means to you. This message will be especially effective when it combines the curiosity and excitement of the child with the skeptical nature of our best scientists, all moderated by the humility of a monk. Your critical thinking then is on display as a pathway to better conclusions. You seek those conclusions not to elevate yourself above those who have other conclusions, but to move us all forward toward some better understanding of who we are. And all the while, you will be improving yourself as a thinker.

Criticism is always a tricky business. In many families and schools, disagreement is identified with meanness. In these settings, the preferred social role is smiling agreement with whatever reasoning is announced. As a critical thinker, you must consider the stark sound of your critical questions in such a context and work self-consciously to make certain that your critical thinking is seen in its best light.

Your best strategy is to present yourself as someone, who like the person who made the argument in the first place is stumbling around, but always watchful for better conclusions. Openness is a central value of a critical thinker, and you show that openness by your eagerness to listen and discover. Whoever finds the better conclusion first is not relevant; what is important is the search for better conclusions. If you give signals to those trying to persuade you that you are their partner in a discovery process intended to enrich you both, they may see your critical questions as a tool that is indispensable to both of you.

Strategies for Effective Critical Thinking

How can you give others the sense that your critical thinking is a friendly tool, one that can improve the lives of the listener and the speaker, the reader, and the writer? Like other critical thinkers, we are always struggling with this question.

Let us conclude this book with a few of the techniques we try to use.

1. Be certain to demonstrate that you really want to grasp what is being said. Ask questions that indicate your willingness to grasp and accept new conclusions.

2. Restate what you heard or read and ask whether your understanding of the argument is consistent with what was written or spoken.

3. Voice your critical questions as if you are curious. Nothing is more deadly to the effective use of critical thinking than an attitude of "Aha, I caught you making an error."

4. Request additional reasons that might enable the person to make a stronger argument than the one originally provided.

5. Work hard to keep the conversation going. If critical thinking is deployed like a bomb, thinking on that topic is halted.

6. Ask the other person for permission to allow you to explore any weaknesses in the reasoning. The idea with this strategy is to encourage the other person to examine the argument with you.

7. Convey the impression that you and the other person are collaborators, working toward the same objective – improved conclusions.

As a parting shot, we want to encourage you to engage with issues. Critical thinking is not a sterile hobby. It provides a basis for a partnership for action among the reasonable. Beliefs are wonderful, but their payoff is in our subsequent behavior. After you have found the best answer to a question, act on that answer. Make your critical thinking the basis for the creation of an identity of which you can be proud. Put it to work for yourself and for the community in which you find yourself.

Index

Ad Hominem argument, 85–86, 94, 101
Advertising:
  ambiguity in, 41–42
  testimonials in, 109–110
Ambiguity, 37–52
  complexity of language and, 38–39
  context and, 43–44
  dictionary definitions and, 44–46
  emotional impact and, 47
  importance of identifying, 52
  limits of your responsibility to clarify, 48
  loaded language and, 46–48
  locating key terms and phrases, 39–40
  in political language, 47–48
  practice exercises, 49–51
  your own writing/speaking and, 48–49
Analogies as evidence, 129–133, 136
  evaluating, 131–133
  generating your own, 132
  importance of evaluating, 133
  practice in evaluating claims supported
    by, 134–136
Appeal to popularity (Ad populum argument),
  89, 101–102
Argument:
  definition/characteristics, 26–27
  evaluating. *See* Critical thinking
Association/correlation *vs.* causation,
  146–147
Assumptions, 53–69, 71–81, 86–88
  defined, 54–55
  descriptive, 71–81
    clues for locating, 74–76, 79
    factual claims as, 105–106
    gap between conclusion and reasons, 74
    identifying with opposition, 75
    identifying with writer/speaker, 75
    illustrating, 72–73
    importance of identifying, 81
    practice exercises, 79–81
  evaluating, 86–88
  general guide for identifying, 55
  vs. incompletely established reasons, 76
  linkage, 56
  multiple conclusions and, 182

  questionable (fallacies), 85–86
  trivial, 78
  value, 53–69
Authorities, appeals to, 89–90, 98, 107,
  110–112, 113, 116
  being in print as a factor, 111
  distorting influences and, 112, 113
  examples of authorities being wrong, 111
  primary *vs.* secondary sources, 112
  research studies. *See* Research studies
    as evidence
Averages, confusing, 156–158. *See also* Statistics

Backward reasoning, 133–134
Begging the question, 96–97
Bias:
  in appeals to authority, 112, 113
  fundamental attribution error, 149
  in observation, research studies, 117–118
  in statistics, 156
  in surveys/questionnaires, 124–126

Case examples as evidence, 128
  importance of evaluating, 136
  practice in evaluating claims supported by,
    134–136
  vs. "striking example", 128
Causation, 137–153
  association *vs.*, 146–147
  evaluating explanation, 149
  multiple contributory causes ("the cause"
    vs. "a cause"), 142
  post hoc fallacy (confusing "after this" with
    "because of this"), 147–149
  practice exercises, 151–152
  rival causes, 137–153, 182
    for detecting, 141
    for differences between groups, 144–145
    evaluating, 150
    importance of finding, 153
    pervasiveness of, 139–141
    search for *vs.* finding possible reasonable
      conclusions, 182
    when to look for (indicators of causal
      thinking), 138